4/96

To Mary Lou —
So glad to be a
member of the same
"club." with you!

Art F Brattoro

Diary of a Small Business Owner

Diary of a Small Business Owner

A Personal Account of How I Built a Profitable Business

Anita F. Brattina

American Management Association

New York • Atlanta • Boston • Chicago • Kansas City • San Francisco • Washington, D.C.
Brussels • Mexico City • Tokyo • Toronto

Library of Congress Cataloging-in-Publication Data

Brattina, Anita F.
    Diary of a small business owner : a personal account of how I
built a profitable business / Anita F. Brattina.
        p.   cm.
    ISBN 0–8144–0291–7
    1. New business enterprises—Case studies.   2. Small business—
Management—Case studies.   3. Entrepreneurship—Case studies.
I. Title.
HD62.5.B73   1995
658.02'2—dc20   95–31947
                                                      CIP

Portions of this book have been reprinted with permission from Inc. magazine,
May and June 1993 issues. Copyright 1993 by Goldhirsh Group, Inc., 38
Commercial Wharf, Boston MA 02110.

Printing number

10 9 8 7 6 5 4 3 2 1

This book is for Bill.

Contents

Diary of a Small Business Owner

Introduction

How It All Began . . .

It has been four months since I made the decision to start my own marketing company and leave W——. Within three weeks of making the decision, I met with our attorney and a friend's accountant. Then I designed some stationery and business cards and bought a new typewriter and had a separate phone line installed in the back bedroom. While my job was falling apart around me (I had a new boss and my job description was being dismantled a little more every day), I was starting Direct Response Marketing. Working on these details kept me interested enough to show up at work. Besides, I needed the paychecks to help fund my start-up.

The climate at work had really been getting worse over the last year. I felt less and less control over my department. The idea of running my own company with no bosses, no board of directors, and no political gamesmanship was more alluring. I had picked my last official day of work and first official day as head of my own consulting firm after reading the employee handbook at W——. If I stayed until March 15 (a three-month wait), I would be eligible for 100 percent instead of 80 percent of W——'s contributions to my pension fund. More start-up capital for the business.

I had chosen marketing consulting because I had seven years' experience in public relations, writing, marketing, and advertising. Also, over the last year I had started helping friends and colleagues around the country with their marketing and advertising questions, which was especially diverting while my position grew tenuous at W——. It felt good to help these small businesses, even if it was for free. If I left W——, I could charge for my time.

But more important than what I wanted to do in my own business, was what I was not going to do. I was not going to work for someone I did not respect. I was not going to have my job description changed without my consent. I was not going to have to worry about corporate politics. I could finally work hard and get rewarded with a fee for my effort. Simple. Pure. I am ready.

My husband, Bill, offered to take me to Myrtle Beach on the Saturday after my last day at W———. And with the greatest pleasure, I put my last few personal things into a box, kissed my secretary, Darlene, goodbye, and walked to my car alone around 4:00 P.M. on Friday. The box went into the basement, I helped Bill put our travel gear into the car, and we left for Myrtle Beach the next morning.

I was dry-eyed as I said goodbye to Darlene. I knew I would see her again because we had become personal friends in the last three months. I had confided in her about the business almost from the day I decided to leave W———. Sometimes we would talk for hours about the different things I could do with the business. She and I became co-conspirators. We even met after work with our husbands and got to know each other better. With Darlene at work and Bill at home, my cheering section was pretty loud. I felt great and never more prepared to venture into the unknown.

I had paid off all our credit cards, socked away more than $15,000 (which included my pension money), had a four-year-old car that was fully paid off and looked brand new. I had a corporate wardrobe that would last me for a few more seasons without major additions. We paid rent on an apartment that was affordable. Bill had only been working in his job for 18 months (he's a medical photographer for one of the city hospitals), but it seemed pretty secure. We didn't have children. I was 27 years old. There couldn't be a better time than this to start a business, I thought.

Years One and Two: Growing Ideas, Getting Started, and Stumbling Around a Little

Year One

Executive Summary

Type of work:	Marketing, direct mail, and telemarketing consulting
Business location:	Second bedroom of our apartment
Number of employees:	None
Sources of new business:	Friends, cold calling
Starting capital:	$8,000 pension-fund distribution
Average monthly sales:	No customers and no prospects. Started from scratch with a few ideas and a list of family, friends, and colleagues
Average sale:	$350
Greatest challenge:	Restraining my enthusiasm
Comments:	More excited about leaving my job than focusing on any one service. My market was anyone who needed marketing or advertising services and who would do business with me.

April 2: Third day on vacation in Myrtle Beach and third day as head of Direct Response Marketing. My days at W—— are behind me. This is not like any vacation I've ever taken.

I'm keeping a notebook of consulting ideas. I could contact someone at the state and offer to teach them how to sell more vanity license plates through a direct mail and telephone campaign, which would generate more revenues for them.

Another business idea: I could go back to the furniture store where we got our sofa last year and sell them a direct mail campaign to get their customers to buy more from them. I'm going to have plenty of work. I will be just fine.

April 4: Talked to Darlene from the hotel. She says flattering things. We only worked together for a year, and yet I feel as if I have known her all my life. She was invaluable to me at the office, understanding exactly what I needed without having to be trained. We were a great team.

Now I'm alone. For a while I'll be doing my own typing and filing and setting my own appointments. But we will continue to see each other as friends. I want us to be on equal footing; I don't want her to be my secretary again. First of all, I could never match her salary and benefits. But more important, I just need to regain control of my own life.

April 6: We'll be home in a few days. The second bedroom is now the corporate headquarters of Direct Response Marketing. I'm going to sit at the desk Bill's mother gave him in high school 23 years ago. I bought an electric typewriter in December, and all the stationery, business cards, and envelopes are sitting in neat piles waiting for me.

I do not have a single customer. But I have lots of ideas, and friends who have told me to call as soon as I was in business full-time. I've been talking to people for four months now. I can't believe it is finally here! I opened up a checking account with $200 from the $8,000 I got from my pension fund. I put the rest in the savings account with our other savings.

April 7: Have I done the right thing? I gave up a very good-paying job. My Buick Skylark has a little over 63,000 miles on it and it's four years old. Maybe I should have bought a new car before I quit. I'm not going to think about it.

So many homes with satellite dishes. Any business opportunities there?

April 10: First day back from Myrtle Beach. Bill has gone to work and I have the rest of the pot of coffee to myself. The apartment is so quiet that I turn on the radio. I can wear jeans. After I finish my to-do list, I'm going to go for a long walk and plan where it is I am going.

LESSONS LEARNED

#1: Getting Started

I've talked with lots of small-business owners, and we all started our businesses for different reasons. Rarely, though, did I meet someone who is still doing exactly and precisely what they planned to do from the very beginning. I think you have to look at the impetus behind a small-business start-up. I made the jump because I felt I was leaving a terrible situation, and starting a business seemed like a fresh alternative. I've met many owners who started businesses because they were laid off, fired, transferred and didn't want to leave the area, had a great business idea but a boss who didn't want to listen, etc. So here we all are—glad to be out of the situation we left and ready to explore this new territory called business ownership.

Many start-up businesses begin with a single customer, someone the owner knew before she quit her job. But many people I've talked to did exactly what I did: started with an idea, no customers, lots of enthusiasm and drive, and an incredible sense of urgency. This momentum carries us through the first few years, when we are doing the most learning.

June 10: It has been two months already, and I do not want to write in this journal. My best work seems to go into business letters to my friends and colleagues, telling them that I've left W—— and have started this business. I've tried to send at least five marketing letters per day. If I read the newspaper and see a company that I think can use my service, I send a letter to them too. Have talked to Darlene almost every day. She tries to avoid W—— as a subject. I tell her what I'm doing. She repeats to me again her idea for a business product we could sell together. She is not interested in a partnership. She just thinks I'm missing an opportunity, but her idea is far from my original intent. It requires producing something. It will mean vendors and deliveries and hiring staff.

My original intent was to specialize in direct mail and telemarketing consulting. So far, no takers. It is different giving advice when you are charging for it. My first client is Pat O. She was the one who told me back in November that I ought to consider starting my own business. So as my way of thanking her, I'm doing four issues of a quarterly newsletter for her business . . . for free. I got the first one pulled together, and it looks great. She loves it. She asked if I would also get it designed and printed, and she would pay the direct costs. No money for me, but it feels good to produce something again. I have my pension money to keep me going.

June 11: I'm still furious over the politics at W—— that forced me to quit. I know I should be glad that it gave me the impetus to start this company, but I can't help feeling betrayed. I never want to have the rug pulled out from under me again. I thought if I just worked hard and kept to myself, I'd be recognized for my contribution. Very naïve.

June 12: After three months, I realize that this is all a little more difficult than I imagined. I want to do really good work, but when I finally get a job like the newsletter for Pat O., I am dependent on the quality of my vendors, like the artist and the printer, and how well I communicate what I want. When I worked with vendors at W——, I was the client but paying with dollars that were not mine. Now every dollar I do not spend wisely is a loss of money for me. I didn't realize how little I knew. I depended on lots of other people to perform my job. Without the staff and resources I am used to, it is very lonely.

I type letters at night after dinner, and in the morning I drive 20 minutes to the business store to make copies of the letters. I see a lot of other people like me at this store. We are the regulars who buy 25 copies of 25 different letters and assorted paper supplies; we have the faces of businesspeople but are dressed in jeans. I would love to stop and talk, but there is no time. Every second I spend away from the phone, I might be missing a phone call from someone who gets my answering machine instead.

During the day, I'm on the telephone following up on my letters and calling new companies to verify names, titles, and addresses for the next round of letters. I think I'm close to getting a few small projects, consulting projects mostly from referrals and friends.

June 14: I talk to Bill's mom and ask her jokingly if she can type. She reminds me that Pat B. (Bill's brother's wife) used to be a secretary with a large insurance company. I will call her tomorrow. If she could type my correspondence and make all the copies, it would free me up to spend more time finding customers. She could also be there to answer the phone.

June 15: Pat said yes . . . and no. She'd be willing to help with typing, but she hasn't done it in ages and is afraid she'll disappoint me. I know her and trust her, so we compromise. I will let her keep my typewriter on her dining-room table, and I'll drive to her house (25 minutes away) to give her correspondence. She'll type it, copy it, and give it to me to sign and mail. We will try it for a few months

---

LESSONS LEARNED

#2: The Isolation of Starting a Business From Home, From Scratch

Moving from the connectedness of a thriving corporation to the isolation of working in the apartment was severe culture shock. No secretary, no phones ringing with incoming business, no using solid years of business to justify instant name recognition, no flood of mail from professional organizations, no phone calls from colleagues sharing ideas. I was also struggling with the realization that executing the idea of this business was much more difficult than coming up with the idea in the first place. I could see quickly that I was floundering, but I was reluctant to admit this to anyone—including Bill.

I wish that I had started out by searching for people who started businesses from scratch and were a few years ahead of me (through networking, trade organizations, chamber of commerce meetings, etc.). Maybe they would have been honest enough to tell me that my two biggest problems were (1) I didn't really know what business I was in, and (2) I had absolutely no direct sales experience or training. I didn't have a clue as to how to sell my business services to the business community. My methods were the ones familiar to me: send letters (I loved to write) and make phone calls (I hated making cold calls and resisted it constantly). I did spend a lot of time calling friends and business associates, who were kind enough to give me referrals and occasional business.

LESSONS LEARNED

#3: Hiring the First Employee

In my previous life in the corporation, I was used to having Darlene to help field phone calls, type, file, and generally help me implement the telemarketing and direct mail programs I designed. But after working from home for a few weeks, doing everything myself, I realized how much time I was losing by trying to do everything alone.

At the very least, I saw myself needing someone to do things that took time (typing, filing, copying, organizing) so that I could sell and service my clients. I had enough money in the bank to seduce myself into thinking I could afford Pat. Actually, her cost to me was less than $60 per week. That freed me to concentrate on selling, which I quickly realized was to be my priority (no clients, so I had to be the one to find the clients). Also, I was not taking Pat away from another employer or asking her to give up health benefits or a pension plan, so she came with as few strings as any employee can have.

I also learned, early in the business, what I liked to do and didn't like to do. I like to meet new people, talk to them about their businesses, and help them implement direct mail and telemarketing campaigns. (I learned later that that is selling, in a fashion.) I don't like detail work, and I hate financial record keeping.

I have been asked by other small-business people how you can afford to take needed money and give it to an employee. My answer is: You have to look at how you are spending your time and what you get back for the investment. I got no return for taking hours out of a day to type and drive to the business center to make copies. I did get a return for spending time finding clients. I believe that the owner has to look at what is the most important task in the company and keep that task for herself.

I learned that most companies are divided into sales and operations. You are either selling the product or creating the product. Usually in a start-up, the single most important thing is sales.

I also believe that new business owners should not hire a salesperson as their first employee. Even if you are horrible at sales, as the owner you should learn a little about the sales process by doing it. That way when you hire your first salesperson, you can tell the salesperson what the customers need to know to make a buying decision.

You can tell her who the best companies are to target. You can tell her what the major objections will be and how to answer those objections. I've seen so many companies flounder because the owner refuses to learn how to sell. Instead, she keeps hiring salespeople and hiding inside the office running operations. I should know. I did it.

and see how it goes. She agrees to work for minimum wage for 10 hours a week to help me out. I know I should look upon her as my first employee, but I see this as a temporary measure. Once business is rolling in, I can talk her into coming aboard full-time. Pat is a very organized, dedicated person. She'll be a tremendous asset to me.

July 4: Independence Day . . . and it feels wonderful to be independent! I have the support of Bill and Pat. Even Darlene is talking about quitting her job at W—— and coming to work for me. She is dead set on trying out this direct mail idea she has. And I'll admit it is looking more attractive as I see how hard it is to sell pure marketing consulting. I also see that I like dealing with tangible things like mailings and phone calls. Selling my ideas—consulting—is hard.

The idea Darlene came up with is a direct mail package we would send to new residents in the county every month. We could sell advertising space in the envelope. I like it because it is tangible. It is something to sell. It has a price tag. In our experience together at W——, we discovered through direct mail testing that the new-resident population is highly responsive to new products and services. This is something I can sell from experience. And it can provide our clients with results that are measurable and attributable to our direct mail program.

I know if we try to launch this idea together, I am putting more responsibility on my shoulders. I've already told Darlene I can't pay her a guaranteed salary. But I have a responsibility to execute her idea well enough that she can match her previous salary through commissions. And I love the idea that Darlene and I can work together again.

I hate working by myself, disconnected from the world.

When I worked at W——, I supervised 50 people, including Darlene, and we worked like an independent company that I managed. I loved that little company. If someone was sick, the work still got done. If I was sick, Darlene was there to step in and take over. We all worked 40–50 hours per week. (Okay, maybe I worked more, but I loved it.)

It would be great to recreate that little company, except with no boss upstairs sending me memos and no board of directors questioning our actions.

July 5: I love it when people ask me what I do and I tell them I own my own business. I can see them look at me in an "oh-then-you-must-be-rich-and-drive-a-Mercedes-and-not-pay-any-taxes" way. If they only knew! It has been four months and I have sent out three invoices totaling less than $1,000.

I'm finding that the small companies need me the most. Direct Response Marketing should help these really small businesses since the larger agencies don't want to deal with them.

July 11: I think Pat might be working from my apartment in a few weeks! She says that when she is sitting at the dining-room table typing, her kids don't respect her. She feels she might be cheating me out of hours because she is interrupted so much! So she will drive to my apartment on Tuesdays and Thursdays and do the correspondence at my apartment. She will also answer the phone.

July 12: I have been working 15-hour days, seven days a week. Bill tries to entice me into doing fun things on the weekends, but they seem like interruptions. When I get a small contract, though, all the work seems worthwhile. There is a purity to it that is hard to explain to someone who doesn't own a business.

But it has also made me moody. Almost every Monday I question this entire decision. One minute I think maybe I should be a clerk at a department store. Then the next moment I get a phone call from someone who wants to meet with me, and I am on a cloud, feeling very professional.

I enrolled in a class that teaches you how to start a business. We meet in the instructor's office one night a week for eight weeks. Our assignment is to write a business plan. I think it's an interesting exercise, but it doesn't seem realistic. I can't connect what I do every day with what I am writing in this plan.

LESSONS LEARNED

#4: Writing Your First Business Plan

Even after being in business for eleven years, I look back on my first business plan and feel sure that it was a waste of time. I was a start-up business with lots of experience in marketing but very little solid business experience. The plan I wrote was as naïve as I was.

Here is what I wish the instructor had forced me to think about: What business are you in, exactly? I find that most floundering businesspeople cannot tell me exactly the business they are in without offering a long-winded explanation. I did the same thing. I wish the instructor had pulled out a Yellow Pages directory and forced me to tell her where I should place my business listing. I wish she had warned me that if I want to list the business under more than one or two headings, my business idea is too vague.

I wish she had helped me to look seriously at the markets I wanted to target. I wish she had discussed my concept as it related to the size of a sale. I wanted to target tiny companies who considered $200 or $300 a lot of money for marketing. It is tough selling a product or service to companies with less than 10 employees, unless the product is very affordable and you have a plan for how to sell a large volume of these products (which means you have to understand selling and the sales process).

I also wanted to sell my services to any company. Now I know that to be successful, I should have targeted a few select types of companies. For example, if I had chosen to specialize in marketing services for dentists, I think I would have been more successful. Once you start targeting a lot of people in the same market, they start talking to each other about you. Also, it is easier to advertise to that audience. The local dental organization has a newsletter, so I could have bought an advertisement in their newsletter, written an article for their newsletter, etc.

In summary: Instead of a business plan, I needed guidance in narrowing my range of services, narrowing the list of business categories I wanted to market, and guidance and ideas about the pricing of my service. I wish she had shown me how many $350 sales I would have to make to earn $100,000 per year and then shown me how to earn $100,000 if I were selling a $10,000 service.

August 15: Thanks to a friend who set up the meeting through the chamber of commerce, I drive to Cleveland and meet Bill W., a man who owns an agency specializing in direct mail. Bill W. is willing to tell me that he has gone through many phases in the last 18 years. Now he is happiest sailing his boat on Lake Erie. He has one employee and talks about his business as though there have been many ups and downs. I can tell I'm on sensitive ground. We spend most of the meeting with my asking him how he does things, how he chooses his vendors, what he does himself.

It seems that he gets most of this income from two or three major clients. He does large mailings for them. The more you mail for a client, the more you make, yet the amount of preparation time for a mailing is relatively the same, regardless of the size of the mailing.

August 16: Talked to George S. (another direct mail shop in Cleveland) by telephone. I realized in both cases that the idea of talking to these guys was good, but I really didn't know the questions to ask. I've made two contacts in a business similar to mine who are not competitors. They seem to be successful. But compared to them, I feel very naïve. George inherited the business from his father, and they have a staff (10 or 15 people, I think). He also has lots of computers and mailing equipment. He is primarily running the shop and has four or five salespeople who bring in the business for him.

September 2: Darlene is joining us! She has agreed to work for free (straight commission) and is bringing her direct mail idea with her.

It's a service we can sell to businesses, who buy space in this special envelope. Together we figured out a name, "Welcome to the Neighborhood." I gathered information on all the costs, set up the pricing, and ordered her business cards. There's no room in the back bedroom for her, but I'll find a place.

I can't believe she is doing this. Am I worth it? I still have about $4,000 left in savings plus zero balances on all my credit cards. We'll have to move fast!

October 1: "Welcome to the Neighborhood" is not selling like hotcakes as we had hoped. Of course, only Darlene is doing the selling, for one to two hours, three days per week. I am paying to print

LESSONS LEARNED

#5: Asking for Advice in the Early Years

My idea of going to another city for advice was a pretty good one. But I could have done a better job asking questions. I was so excited about the business owners being willing to talk, I didn't bother worrying about how successful they were. If I were going to do it over again, I would have asked my friend to track down companies with at least 15 employees where the founder is still running the company. To me, 15 employees can't be supervised by the owner alone. So he must have learned how to delegate too. Only from successful founders will you get honest answers about the early years and about what they really did to be successful. I'd rather spend a day with one successful founder than a whole room full of corporate executives. Successful founders are part of a special club. To find them, ask every president you meet: "Oh, did you start this company?" and "How many employees do you have?" Now, there are lots of very savvy presidents who did not found their companies. I'm not saying you can't learn something from them. But founders who have built companies and gotten them over the hump of $2–5 million in sales will be able to provide key pieces of information about every stage of their company's growth.

The questions. When you meet with one of these founders, ask:

"How did you start this business?"

"What were the keys to your successfully growing this business?"

"What successful methods have you used to find new customers?"

"What is your average sale?"

"In the early years, were you more involved in sales or operations?"

"Who did you hire to cover the side you were not covering?"

"What was your background and business experience?"

"What were the three things you did that most helped you grow this business?"

"Can I keep in touch with you from time to time and ask you questions about problems I am encountering?"

LESSONS LEARNED

#6: Beginning to Understand the Sales Process

Since I was a novice at sales, I was relieved that Darlene was willing to join the company and help me with this aspect, even if it meant changing the focus of the company and adding this new service. That's how afraid I was of selling.

What I didn't know then and I know now is that the sales process is divided into four steps. A friend taught me this from his 15 years in sales. According to him, these are the sales steps:

1. Getting the customer's attention
2. Building interest in your product
3. Desire by the customer
4. Action by the customer

Most of us owners with no previous sales experience are pretty good at explaining our service or product (building interest). But we hate cold calling (getting the customer's attention), we are unfamiliar with noticing buying signals (desire), and we are usually not good at getting the customer to sign a contract (action) and discuss terms and financial arrangements of the sale.

If more owners could figure out which of the four steps they were good (and bad) at, they could work on their skills. Understanding these four steps can also help you assess the sales skills of your salespeople.

For example, Darlene was wonderful at cold calling and getting appointments. I was terrible at it. So she actually was a breakthrough for me. She helped me to get in front of more businesses. I think she was instrumental in building my business for the first three years because she was so good at that part. In the early years, she was not as good as I was when it came to observing buying signals (desire) or getting contracts signed (action). I learned those two steps quickly because I was so desperately learning how to make money and prove that this decision to start a business was a good one. If I had taught her those two steps, she would have been a wonderful salesperson for the company.

Instead, she helped me with my greatest weakness (cold calling/getting the customer's attention). I slowly learned the other three steps, because if I didn't learn them I would starve.

Now I tell business owners that if they want to get more business, they should employ telemarketing (use a service like the one my company provides, or hire their own) to help them get appointments. Then they can get sales training to teach them how to look for buying signals (desire) and how to ask for the order (action). Once they have figured out the whole process, it is time to hire and train a salesperson to do the same thing.

the envelopes and ads and mail it, which is very expensive (I never realized it could cost more than $2,000 just for one mailing), as well as continuing to sell our consulting services. Darlene also got a part-time job to tide her over until the commission checks start coming in. And I am getting some consulting contracts from the people she meets who don't really need "Neighborhood" but rather more full-scale marketing.

To make it work, we have to talk to 500 businesses, get 50 appointments, and convert 15 into contracts—every month. Darlene is calling businesses out of the Yellow Pages.

October 16: I have been helping Darlene sell this product with a fixed price tag ("Welcome to the Neighborhood") for the last two weeks. She is actually better than me at getting the appointments. But I am better at getting them to sign a contract and write a check. I realize that I know very little about sales and am afraid of rejection at that first meeting. Darlene is not afraid of anyone. We had an appointment the other day with the head of marketing of a large utility company. I was nervous the entire day before the appointment. And what does Darlene talk to him about for the first half hour? Fertilizer! Comparing notes on how they get their lawns green. They trade fertilizer brand names, and then John starts the meeting.

How can I be afraid of anyone again? I'll just imagine them carrying fertilizer to their car. Maybe the secret of sales is just not worrying about yourself so much.

October 19: Darlene hates being paid on straight commission. I think she would work just as hard even if paid her a fixed salary, but I can't afford it. She wants to see her ideas well executed, and she wants recognition for her efforts. She doesn't like a lot of rules and reports. Pat, on the other hand, likes more structure and ritual.

She likes doing the same things every day. She doesn't like making big decisions alone. Dar loves it.

October 20: What do I find hard to do? I dislike talking to someone if I think I will be rejected. I dislike confrontation. If someone is not doing what I want, I have a hard time telling them directly.

I am not as organized as I used to think I was at W——.

What am I extremely good at now?

I can hear about someone's business, ask a few key questions, and invariably be able to diagnose their marketing problems. I love meeting new people (clients) if I think that they want to see me and that I am able to construct programs such that people are willing to buy them. I'm a good writer and can write marketing recommendations quickly and easily. I like juggling multiple tasks. I'm fairly quiet and like to listen to others. I believe I can accomplish anything I want to accomplish.

October 22: I've decided I'm going to stop telling people I own a business. They assume I'm successful, when I am far from it.

October 23: I'm a guest in a "start your own business" class at the community college. The teacher from the class I took in July invited me. I do enjoy speaking to people like this. I also realize that I have to keep up my skills. At W—— I was on hundreds of mailing lists for information, trade journals, newsletters, etc. Now that I work from my home, I miss seeing all that mail. I had to go to the library and do research for my talk.

November 1: John N. called. He was a student in the "start your own business class" and wants to hire us to help him develop a marketing plan for his company!

November 2: Darlene and I sit down to figure out how to make money in this business. Right now our average sale is $350. So if we want to generate $250,000 in sales for the year, we have to make 714 sales. If we want to generate $150,000, we have to generate 429 sales. With Darlene's help, "Neighborhood" is bringing in about eight sales per month (96 per year), and I'm bringing in about $1,500 per month in consulting work from "Neighborhood" customers. We have to make a lot more sales per month!

November 5: Today I negotiated a rent-free one-year lease for about 500 square feet of space in a hotel near the apartment. I made the decision after meeting with a magazine ad salesman in my living room last week. Alone. Nervous. I don't feel as if I'm really in business. Besides, the printer has a tough time delivering all our supplies for "Neighborhood" to the apartment every month, and I want to hire people to help us stuff the envelopes instead of Bill, Darlene, and me doing it at the dining-room table. We can afford to pay $100–$200 per month for mailing help from some of Darlene's neighbors so that Bill doesn't have to stuff envelopes anymore.

We will be in a hotel in the heart of the business district in a suburb. In exchange, I've offered to produce a nice brochure for the hotel (Bill is going to take the photographs). Then we will pay $300 per month for the next two years if we decide to stay. The office is humble, but it's easy to get around, close to other businesses, and right next door to the local chamber of commerce. To afford this move and pay for the brochure we promised to create for our landlord, we need to increase our billings by another $2,000 a month. That is seven more "Neighborhood" contracts per month, or one or two more consulting projects.

February 19: Over the holidays no one seemed to want to talk about business, so I concentrated on pulling together a mailing list for our "Neighborhood" program. If this happens every holiday, these slow times will be hard on us once we have the overhead of the office (we move in a few weeks). Darlene took time off to be with her family in December. We have high hopes for the coming year.

Last night Darlene and I brought our husbands to the new office. They didn't say much. This is our project, and they really are not a part of it. Right now the offices look a little threadbare (they are former hotel rooms in the office section of this suburban hotel), but Darlene and I have already picked out paint colors and have ideas about used furniture and plants. We are coming in next weekend to work on it.

My savings are gone. I am now using credit cards. I have enough to pay Darlene $1,000 per month for the next few months so that she can quit her other part-time job and come work for me full-time. Once she is here full-time and has her own office and her own telephone, she will be able to bring in much more business.

From reviewing our past ten months of sales and our marketing opportunities, "Neighborhood" can be our greatest opportunity for growth. It is a developed program, and our customers love it. It really does get them more business than other direct mail programs they've used.

I also need a new car and a computer. Our cash flow is terrible. We owe about $4,000 in bills (mostly printing bills from "Neighborhood") and have $2,000 with which to pay the bills and almost nothing in outstanding money owed to us. I just have to go out and sell more. Instead of selling the $350 "Neighborhood" package, I need to be selling a $1,000 package. Perhaps we need to redesign the program for our larger customers, who really want to be in all the zip codes anyway. Maybe I could concentrate on those accounts.

February 27: Feel as if I'm walking up ten flights of stairs carrying a hundred overloaded briefcases, two bags of groceries, and a basket of wet laundry. I am working every waking hour, and it is still not enough. I'm moving us into this office and making commitments to Darlene for more money, and I don't have it. But I don't see any other way to do this. I still have the credit cards.

March 19: We moved into our new offices. There's a lot we still need, but with some used furniture we had at home and a few garage sales, the place looks grand. It's a far cry from my office at W——: no silver jug for ice water, no $350 executive chair, but it is our first office. Darlene started full-time on Monday. I also hired an intern, Carol M. She has no experience in marketing, but she doesn't cost us anything. She will be our inside production person, helping to coordinate the jobs and get "Neighborhood" in the mail on time. Pat will answer the phones, do the billings, and our correspondence. Pat is still working part-time. I am going to try hard to concentrate on sales.

March 20: Thank heaven for understanding suppliers. If we hadn't gotten an extra extension on credit from our vendors, we would have gone out of business when S—— did not pay their $5,000 bill for 90 days, and when this brochure we agreed to do for the hotel cost more than I ever anticipated. The free rent is looking a lot less "free."

March 29: Ouch. We got our first real phone bill at the higher, commercial rates. Commercial was the only way to get a listing in the Yellow Pages. $375 versus $75 at home.

March 30: The end of one year in business. It has been quite a year. From all the calls we've made, letters we've mailed, and the newsletter we sent out, we are getting requests for information about our services weekly. Mostly the calls are for "Welcome to the Neighborhood." I still find it hard to put in less than a 12- to 14-hour day, yet Bill and I have never gotten along better. Tomorrow we are leaving for Myrtle Beach for a one-week vacation with good friends. Bill is paying for it. He doesn't know how broke we really are.

End of Year One

Year Two

Executive Summary

Type of work: "Neighborhood" direct mail program, custom direct mail production, marketing consulting, design services

Business location: 500 square feet in a suburban hotel

Number of employees: 2

Sources of new business: Referrals, word of mouth, speaking engagements regarding direct mail and telemarketing, newsletter to chamber of commerce mailing list and to assorted business cards collected at meetings, prospecting by people with no previous sales experience

Capital needs: Spent entire pension fund, and capitalized using a variety of personal credit cards obtained while still employed at previous job.

Average monthly sales: $10,000 by the end of the year

Average sale: $800

Annual revenue: Approx. $100,000

Greatest challenge of the year: Dealing with cash flow

Comments: Realizing that I do not know as much about the production process as I thought. Also contending with managing and getting work done through others, mostly people with no previous experience in the industry.

22

May 22: Darlene talked to Burt R. about advertising in "Neighborhood" and suggested he talk to me since he needed other marketing. He is a very successful businessman who owns a chain of franchise stores. He keeps his lifetime goals on a piece of yellow paper folded up in his wallet. Is that what it takes to become successful?

June 23: Went home to watch my sister, Eileen, graduate from art school. I'd promised her that if she graduated I would hire her in the business. So she knows she has a job. She still has a lot of growing up to do, but she is mature in lots of ways too. She's going to live with us for a while and then get her own apartment. I still am not taking a salary, but a promise is a promise. Besides, right now we are using outside freelance artists, so the cost to hire Eileen is not that much more than our current expense. Since everyone works part-time except Darlene and me (and we're out on sales calls a lot), Eileen is one more person to answer the phones.

July 15: Eileen has moved in and is handling all the artwork in the business. There is only enough money to pay her barely above minimum wage, and only part-time. So she will live with us a little while longer to keep her expenses down. Bill is a saint for putting up with all of this.

I am also realizing that selling services $350 at a time is asking for trouble. I have raised the price of "Neighborhood" and offered advertisers a broader geographic area. Now the minimum price is $850; prices go all the way up to $10,000. We have lost some of our smaller advertisers, but overall we are making a little more money and don't need to make as many sales per week to hit our sales goals.

[Personal note: we are looking for our first home. There is low-interest money available to first-time home buyers. With all of these struggles with the business, I'd like to have something to show for it.]

To really make this business work, pay everyone full-time wages plus benefits, and take home $30,000 per year, we need to be generating $40,000 in sales every month. That means hiring six people who will each generate $7,000 per month in sales. (If our average contract is $850, that is 8.5 sales per month, or a little over two sales per week. Darlene could run the sales staff, and Pat and Carol could run the office staff.

We are sending out our second newsletter. People seem to love it, and we have gotten a few new customers from the first one we mailed last year.

July 30: Started using a new company to help Eileen execute her designs into artwork the printer can use for our direct mailing projects.

Sometimes I sit and talk to Bill K. about business. He has an office half the size of ours in a shopping center near where we go to get our copies made every day. He has one employee and seems to get by with very little typing, answers his own phone, and does his own invoicing. He has one account that he bills about $8,000 per month. Then accounts like me are just extra money. He's not even friendly all the time (when he's got a deadline looming for his major client), so I can't imagine him selling every day the way I do. I guess we all find our own way to be in business in this world. His way makes me nervous. I'd be fearful that my big client would go belly up.

To make our business successful, we must sell "Welcome to the Neighborhood" in greater volumes. I must take the time to train Darlene on how to sell and handle objections and get contracts, or we're not going to make it. Even though I don't have any sales experience, I can see that Darlene struggles when it comes to asking for the order. You need to get the customer to tell you they think your program is a good idea. Then you have to suggest a trial contract of some kind. Darlene feels uncomfortable with that step. Maybe I need to give her greater incentives to sell.

Dar offered to resign today. Said that she couldn't pay her bills with what she was making and that she had two boys who were heading for college in a few years. I talked her out of it. I feel responsible for her low sales. I must not be supporting her enough.

August 6: Sometimes I let the business overwhelm me to the point I get totally self-absorbed and forget my vision. I must never lose sight of the fact that it doesn't matter what business we are in; I must figure out a consistent way to sell that particular service and make money. If we are not making enough money, nothing else matters.

September 4: We finally found a house! It's got a huge yard and we can make the mortgage payment even if I work at McDonald's. When we were filling out the mortgage application, the man asked me what I did. I told him I was self-employed and he asked me for how long. I told him about 18 months. He suggested I write "housewife" as my occupation.

September 5: A good friend is in charge of a program helping women reentering the job market after raising children, a divorce, etc. Carol M. came to us from her program. I am hiring four of these women as intern/salespeople. DRM doesn't pay anything for them. I will teach them, along with Darlene, to be salespeople . . . how to each bring in five new "Neighborhood" accounts at $1,000 each. They will earn a 20 percent commission. Darlene and I are just not bringing in enough business. If these women don't cost the company anything and I can train them properly, they could help generate $50,000 per month in steady income to the business. If we can get this launched, we will be doing wonderfully!

September 9: We have five salespeople, and I have finally gotten our pricing onto one sheet of paper and narrowed down our general marketing services to about a dozen services. This way, if one of them is out selling "Neighborhood" and they run into someone who needs something else, they've got the prices in front of them. The bad part of all this is that with so many new employees, it is hard to pay attention to my regular customers. The salespeople need so much attention, especially because none of them have previous sales or marketing experience. But didn't Mary Kay Ash take the same kind of women and turn them into super-salespeople through training, motivation, and incentives? I can do the same thing. I am going to help them be successful.

September 10: After a very tense day, I sat down and drew an organizational chart of our company on a tablet. I also wrote job descriptions for everyone. This is self-defense. Everyone comes to me with questions, and I can't do my own work. I need to tell everyone what I think they should be doing in writing. I think it will cut down on all the questions I am getting continually. Bill says I need to delegate more. I've come to realize that even though I've been in management for many years, I really do not understand delegating or do it well. So I must learn to adhere to the job descriptions I've written, support every decision my employees make, reward good work through officewide recognition, and say "I don't know" "What do you think is the best thing to do?" and "I'll back your decision whatever it is."

September 29: I'm already thinking that having all of these sales-people is a bad idea. We just have to go after larger accounts. If each salesperson brought in $18,000–$20,000 instead of $7,000, then five salespeople could bring in $100,000 per month. Wow!

Maybe we really need to expand as a full-service advertising agency to increase our average sale.

September 30: Money, money, money. I spend 99 percent of my energy worrying about the fact that I have so little of it. Solution: Go into sales full-time. I can't wait for these inexperienced sales-people anymore.

With so many employees, I'm trapped in the office answering questions and putting out fires. Darlene and I barely see each other. Pat just sticks to the basics: answering the phones, helping send out invoices, doing typing, and helping where she is needed. Eileen is doing the artwork and working with Bill K. Her artwork is uneven. Sometimes it is incredible and the client loves it. Sometimes it looks so amateurish I want to cringe, and I make her do it over, which we both hate. Carol tries hard to keep the "Neighborhood" mailings on schedule. But mostly, she asks me lots of questions and seems to hate making decisions on her own.

The other salespeople sit at telephones in the office (I had to put in more lines), and one person is sitting at a typewriter stand in the hallway, but we all fit. Pat laughs and says we don't need staff meet-ings. She sits in the middle of us all and can hear absolutely every conversation in the office. These new salespeople hate making sales calls. I've given them each a phone book and a list of the companies that will be interested in "Neighborhood" and a script guideline. They look sad a lot and get up to refill coffee cups frequently.

October 26: Bill's birthday is next week. He has been so wonderful that I am going to surprise him and take him to a golf resort in New Jersey to go golfing for the weekend. He deserves it. I've been ignoring him for months.

At work, I still have to bring in more business myself. I find myself caught up in being a coach and putting out fires for the clients we already have. I think we might be underpricing our services. Maybe if I had a bookkeeper (which I can't afford), she could look at these prices and tell me whether I'm always broke because I'm not charging enough or because I don't have enough sales. I seem to be doing everything. It's as if I'm in charge and am surrounded by people who can't do anything unless I give them instructions.

October 28: I am running this business by the skin of my teeth. If I can't get these salespeople to sell something, they are going to put me under. Technically they are free since they are on straight commission, but the resources they absorb are my time, Pat's time, Darlene's time, phone bills, postage, and brochure inventory. I thought I could develop this crack team of salespeople and deploy them and they would bring back business. But it has been two months and it is not working.

October 29: Okay. I owe $15,000 in due bills and have $200 in the checking account. We have about $10,000 in invoices owed to us. First, I take all the due bills and put them in date order so I can see what needs to be paid first. Then I have to contact all these creditors and work out payment arrangements and tell them what is going on. Send partial payments if necessary. Then trim all expenses to the bare bone. Relook at the situation with all of these "free" salespeople. Design a plan to bring in accounts with a larger profit margin. Set a minimum monthly sales quota. Communicate it to everyone ($5,000?). If it is not met, ask them to leave.

November 5: Car trouble. Sitting in the donut shop parking lot waiting for Pat's husband to come get me. I thought I didn't have any control when I was a marketing executive at W——; this is totally out of control. I can't get to my appointments. I don't really have the money to fix the car. When Joe picked me up I really lost my composure. "What have you learned from this?" Joe asks. I am stunned. I want to tell him my problems, but he is not paying attention. He is right in a way; I can only start figuring out what to do next. I got myself into this mess; I'm going to have to get myself out of it.

I ask my neighbor to look at the car. He fixes it for under $50.

November 18: We are a step closer to getting the house. I think we will close on the mortgage by Christmas! I have cut back the hours of our intern/salespeople, and Dar and I have taken over the selling again. I still seem to be the best person to get someone to sign a contract. Dar is maintaining a flow of $5,000 in business each month and I'm bringing in the remaining $15,000 per month through contracts for direct mailings, consulting, and miscellaneous advertising (we did get the contract with Burt R. to help him with direct mail and advertising for his chain of stores).

November 24: Bill and I were walking through the mall shopping for Christmas when all of a sudden I became so overwhelmed with despair that I could barely breathe. Bill bought us some coffee and I finally told him how bad things were. We have too many employees, we are struggling financially, I can't pay our bills, I have tapped out our credit cards, and now we are taking on the mortgage.

He took it very well. First he reminded me that lots of people talk about starting businesses, but few people actually do it. Second, we have accumulated some great clients and have done some outstanding marketing work. Third, every time I see a problem, I'm able to fix it, and he is confident I can work through this problem too. Fourth, he can handle the mortgage payment and assures me that the problems will work out.

LESSONS LEARNED

#7: The Rewards of an Understanding Spouse

Throughout every low point in the business, when I felt like talking, Bill was there; I could talk to him and bounce ideas off him. He was strong and stable and reasonable when I felt out of control. I don't feel I could have built the business to where it is without the support system he provided.

He urged me to get a handle on the business finances and get Pat's help to track all our income and expenses. He's right. We need to set up internal cost controls on each project so that we can see what we are spending while we are spending it, not after. I must make this business work.

November 25: Another long day. But today I feel differently. That's because more than $4,000 in checks came in today. That did a lot to reduce my stress level. In selling, we are down to Darlene, Maggi (one of the "free" salespeople), and me. The other four women are either gone or coming in to type their resumes in their job search. Carol and Eileen are struggling with running operations while I go back outside and sell. This is hard, because the reality is this is the first job either of these women has ever had in marketing.

November 29: Thanksgiving Day is in a few hours, and I can't sleep. I read an article about E. B. White in a magazine. The author said that White had led a charmed life. Said he had married happily, had a wonderful childhood, was successful at a young age, and was in demand as a writer all his life. He lived most of it with his family in a farmhouse in the country. That sounds so perfect. Someone in America really did live that way. So it is possible. And what is the difference between E. B. and me? A charmed life. I'd like a taste of that someday.

LESSONS LEARNED

#8: Salespeople—Free and Otherwise

I have not yet met an owner who successfully hired and maintained a "commission only" sales force. Now I recommend offering a base salary of at least $1,000 to $1,500 per month. I also recommend that sales goals represent six to fifteen times the salesperson's monthly expense to you (depending on the profit margins in your industry). Remember that sales expenses include commissions on top of base salary, automobile, parking and tolls, telephone, postage, entertainment expenses, and tax contributions.

December 8: This past week I feel I've grown up. First, I finally figured out an internal bookkeeping system that I can manage and understand and teach to Pat. Good, bad, or indifferent, at least I can see how we are doing every week.

December 15: We closed on our house three days ago! We really own something solid and immovable. The monthly payments are so low that we could afford to make them even if both Bill and I were working at minimum-wage jobs.

December 18: I never thought I would ever fall asleep in front of the television, yet I find myself doing it regularly these days. I'm filling every waking hour with something to do until I reach a level of exhaustion so complete, I drop off to sleep. I guess I'm afraid of my own random thoughts.

Resolution for the new year: Don't hire a salesperson unless they can get appointments using the telephone. I can teach them to sell face-to-face later if they master the first skill. If they can't persuade people by phone, then they'll probably never sell anything face-to-face.

January 5: I went to a "start your own business" conference and heard two guys make business finance sound easy. They explained break-even analysis in a way I could finally understand. Mainly they describe a way to list all my expenses so that I can figure out my direct expenses and indirect expenses very month. I think I can do this. They say to be careful when money is flowing in smoothly. You might be tempted to increase your overhead, and then, if things suddenly slow down, you can get into serious trouble. But my car has over 110,000 miles on it, and I don't think it is going to make it through the winter.

Saw Barb M. at the conference. We haven't talked since college graduation. She's managing her family's moving company and is trying to learn all she can about business finances. We agree to try meeting for lunch on some regular basis.

January 8: I'm now working seven days a week, about 65 hours per week. About 45 hours are at the office; the rest are at home.

January 24: Eileen and I talked again. She's been working for me for six months now, and I am not sure what to do with her. She

LESSONS LEARNED

#9: Hiring Relatives as Employees

I employed Pat, my sister-in-law, and Eileen, my sister. Pat had previous office experience; Eileen did not. I thought it was possible to work with family. But I was doing Eileen a favor by guaranteeing her her first job. If she had come to us with some office experience, the situation would probably have been better.

I asked Eileen recently if she is glad she worked for me. She remembers it as an emotional experience that was mostly bad. And I was emotional, because I was scared to death that I was going to take us into bankruptcy.

Eileen says she doesn't remember me acting in an emotional manner. In fact, she admits that she never knew I was under any pressure at all. I was good, I guess, at hiding my fear and appearing to be cool. Today, I think I'm less emotional because I have stronger business skills. I think I still appear cool, even when I'm ruffled. It's a habit that protected me from too many questions from employees or clients or family members.

seems unhappy all the time. I know I'm tougher on her because she is my sister. But I want her to be better than anyone else. And it is hardest when she doesn't follow the rules I ask everyone else to follow. But her design ideas can be brilliant, and she is great with clients. Why did I get myself into this?

February 12: Carol told me she wants to cut her hours this summer to be with her son. I know she is a single mother, but I ask her what her first priority is. She insists that it's her son, Brian. She suggests job sharing. I know she is frustrated in her job and I try to think of a solution, but job sharing is not a good one. I knew when I started that I could only afford to hire the most inexperienced help, but I believed that I could train them. Maybe that won't work anymore. I really want someone in Carol's job with more production experience.

Started using a woman named Liza B. to do the typesetting for our direct mail when Bill K. was too busy with his major client.

LESSONS LEARNED

#10: Understanding the Relationship Between Payables, Receivables, and Payroll in a Service Business

For the first four years in business, I struggled with poor cash flow. I did the same for the next four years, but for different reasons. When I started, I was underpricing my services. Therefore my accounts payable were usually the same as or more than my receivables. Now I know this is often an indicator that either pricing is too low or overhead is too high, or both.

The second four years I rarely had cash, but my receivables were three to five times my payables. I was pricing properly, I was selling well, but we were growing so fast that before I could get paid for one job, we were already expanding payroll to work on the next project. In the second situation, banks would have loved to lend me operating capital or start a line of credit to help me through the times when I needed cash to meet payroll and pay bills.

In the situation of the first four years, I was a poor credit risk and I had poor cash flow. In the second four years, I had poor cash flow, but for good business reasons. We were growing: All in all, I didn't understand the critical relationship between receivables and payables, and didn't ask anyone else who was savvy enough to tell me if I was doing anything wrong. Of course, I never had the nerve to ask for advice in those days, so how could I have known?

She's been in the marketing business for more than 15 years, and I've been telling her my problems. She's given me some great advice. It would be nice to have someone like her around to replace Carol, but I can't afford Liza yet.

February 16: I met with an accountant from the firm that helped me get my tax identification number two years ago. She's on her own now and is going to be our new accountant. I haven't used anyone in the interim because I couldn't afford it. But now I want help to set up those ledger sheets that the men talked about in that business finance seminar. That way I can see what is happening with our accounts more easily, and Pat can help me track those numbers.

In reviewing our financial history with the accountant, I'm shocked to see how much money I have spent. All together so far I have invested $12,000 of our savings and about $15,000 in credit cards toward the business. The accountant said that someday I can take that money out of the business. Then I'll do something with it to help me feel all this sweat was worth it.

She says I don't really owe my employees a job. They must do what I ask, or I will have to find people who can do it. She also says we must watch our billings very carefully. She suggested asking for 50 percent deposits before we start work. We must not let clients go more than 30 days with unpaid bills before we say something. Get Pat's help with this? I hate calling customers about money. I must start paying myself (I told her that was in my plans as soon as we had the money).

I didn't tell her that my other big concern is the work we are producing. We are doing everything ourselves, and I want it to be so much better. But I entrust it to Carol and Eileen, and then I get angry when they don't do it exactly the way I would do it. Then I have them do it over, without any extra charges to the client, of course. But it eats away at the profit. I want them to think on their own, have higher standards than mine, know the right thing to do without asking me. My problem is I have a staff of people who all like each other and get along really well. Letting anyone go would affect morale. It would also mean I'd have to replace them immediately, and fill in myself, until the new person got up to speed.

February 18: Horrible week. Carol missed another deadline, and I lost my temper. (When I peel away all the excuses, I see she really is so inexperienced.) She's walking around looking pained. I had a fight with Eileen. She can't seem to prioritize her work. Much crying. I find her resignation letter on my desk under a pile of papers. I talk her out of it. Maggi comes in and informs me she will set up appointments for me but not for Darlene, because she doesn't want to be anyone's secretary. This is a very long week.

February 20: Talked to one of my clients about what is going on. He says that we are experiencing growing pains. So if this is growth, what do I really have to worry about?

LESSONS LEARNED

#11: Hiring and Firing When You Are Tiny and Have No Backup

This is one of the worst situations I had to confront. What do you do when you can see your employee screwing up and you know you could do it yourself, do it better, and do it in one-fifth the time. Yet you can't even shave another 15 minutes out of the day to relax, so how are you going to take on that whole job if you eliminate that person? And how do you hire someone behind her back?

In the early years, I'm not sure there is a solution. Except perhaps to hire the most experienced person for the job that you can afford. I think if I had really searched, I could have found more experienced help and paid relatively the same. Then I would have had to face fewer hiring/firing decisions. My problem was, I hired spontaneously. If I liked someone, I hired them. I never weighed experience into the equation. I know: dumb.

---

1. That jobs get done properly. So: After Carol leaves, hire Liza or someone experienced like her to handle production. Liza has 20 times more experience.
2. I will burn out from trying to do sales and operations. So: Get Dar and Maggi to take more responsibility for managing their accounts after the sale.
3. Costs. We can't cover our expenses because we didn't price the job properly. So: Give Carol the job of analyzing all our jobs costs again.
4. Not enough new business coming in. So: Get Darlene and Maggi each up to $10,000 per month through training.
5. People not knowing what is going on. So: Have planned production meetings every week.

I've been reading about entrepreneurs who have become successful. Maybe we're not doing as badly as I think. We've now done about 100 jobs. We have established our name in the city. We have not gone outside to borrow money. We've treated our employees fairly. We are renting offices that are comfortable and usable. We have most of the proper equipment, and what we don't have we can rent or subcontract. We have established good client contacts and are doing good work. We have identified the services that we do well in a basic price range that our clients can afford. I am doing very little consulting. Mostly we are helping people with direct mail projects plus doing "Welcome to the Neighborhood" every six weeks. (I stretched out the time between editions to save money and give us more time to sell the advertising space.) We have developed an organization and systems within it to handle most jobs.

We have a ways to go, but we'll be okay.

February 23: Buick died with more than 120,000 miles and a cracked engine block. Bought a new Dodge Colt sedan off the showroom floor. Negotiated a great price at 9:45 P.M., and drove the car home. Just bought five more years of transportation at a price we can handle. When I first started this, I thought I'd be driving an expensive foreign car in 12 months. Now that I know what I've gotten into, I'd rather not have the expensive-foreign-car payments. I'll know when I'm ready for that.

February 24: Bill has gone off to Deep Creek with Darlene's husband and a couple of other guys. I have the weekend alone. Mostly I want to sleep. Carol made it official. She is leaving as of June 1. I talked to Liza. She wants $36,000 per year. We can't afford her. But she said she'd help me interview candidates to replace Carol.

Eileen and I had another fight yesterday about the job she managed for N——, one of our clients. Then R—— was upset over a typo that was on their direct mail piece. Then Pat's husband said he could not take our mail to the post office anymore, so that's one more thing I'll have to do. Then J. (a client) took me to lunch and informed me he had found a new life and that I needed to renounce the devil in my heart. I definitely need to crawl into bed.

Went out to dinner with Eileen. We talked like friends, instead of sisters ready to kill each other. I am seven years older than she is. She is still my baby sister. But we do know that we are capable of producing great artwork together. If only we could do it without fighting!

March 1: On Friday I had a really interesting meeting with Ellice J., a highly successful sales representative for an employment agency.

She called on me for business, and we ended up agreeing to have lunch together. I like her because she is so enthusiastic about her work, and she loves to sell! She started working for this agency 10 years ago and is paid a very low guaranteed salary (similar to what I pay Darlene) and then a "generous" commission structure (she doesn't think it is generous). But she discovered early on that she loved to sell and was good at it. She probably makes $75,000 a year (I'm not really sure). She also goes to a sales psychiatrist, so to speak, a sales trainer who keeps her excited and motivated. She pays for him herself. She is the first person I have met who loves to sell. What would happen if I were like her? What would happen if Darlene were like her?

March 2: Went to see Phil B., a prospective client. Met him at a friend's party. Like Ellice, he is a successful sales representative (for an insurance agency). He probably makes over $100,000 a year. Phil B. and Ellice J. are two of the most ambitious salespeople I've ever met. They both generate more than $1 million in annual sales for each of their employers. I am upset because Darlene can't bring in $100,000 a year in business. What would happen if I had someone like Phil or Ellice working for our company?

Phil likes what he hears and wants me to meet his boss, Charlie F.

March 19: Eileen is definitely leaving so that we can stay friends and sisters. Carol M. is leaving this summer to spend more time with her son. Dar and Maggie need to maintain a steady flow of new business. So do I.

March 27: Bill and I talked last night. I have to make this business successful. Then my reward will be to take a little time off, cut back on my hours, and raise some children. But to do that I am going to need a production chief (Liza?), and a graphic artist to replace Eileen. I would also need another writer besides me, and a full-time bookkeeper, and very competent account executives to bring in business and service those accounts.

The fact is, I still bring in the bulk of the business. And I service all the business. And as long as that continues, I'll never be able to have children. So what do I need to teach Maggi and Darlene? They are good at getting appointments and getting in front of people. But once they are with the prospective customer, they don't know what to do. They need to concentrate on asking the right questions and correctly assessing needs. That's all I do. I don't really sell. I just listen to people's business problems and write them a prescription. They feel that it will work for them, they say okay, and we get business.

March 28: Today I am in serious need of $5,000 to meet payroll and pay some bills. I always read that the problem with small companies is cash flow. The problem with us is we need $5,000. Actually, we need about $15,000. It is coming from our clients, but it is all on paper. By April 15, if everyone pays their bills, we'll have $16,300.

Our company anniversary is in three days. It's time to look at where I have led the company. I am uncomfortable most of the time. Cash flow is terrible. The skill levels of my employees doesn't come anywhere near my own. I can't sleep at night. My conclusion is that "Welcome to the Neighborhood" is my problem. It is a mailing program we designed that relentlessly needs to go in the mail every six weeks, regardless of the number of advertisers in the envelope. In looking at our customers, I think I can convince many of our regular "Neighborhood" customers to continue a similar mailing that would cost a little more but would yield even better results. I would be able to stop the monthly printing and postage bills that have been piling up. Our monthly sales would drop, but so would our fixed costs.

End of Year Two

Years Three
and Four:
Hiring Experts

Year Three

Executive Summary

Type of work:	Direct mail production, design, tele-marketing consulting, marketing consulting, mailing lists
Business location:	500 square feet in suburban hotel
Number of employees:	7 (mostly part-time)
Sources of new business:	Referrals, word of mouth, attending professional and chamber meetings, newsletter, telemarketing for appointments
Investment capital:	Personal credit cards
Average monthly sales:	$18,000
Average sale:	$1,000
Annual revenues:	Approx. $220,000
Greatest challenge of the year:	Hiring lots of inexperienced help and paying the consequences
Comments:	Confronting my lack of business skills and the belief that if one salesperson can bring in $4,000 per month, then five salespeople could bring $20,000

April 2: Told the staff I was ending the "Neighborhood" program at a specially called staff meeting. Instead, I told everyone, we would market our direct mail, design, and mailing services, and I would also do direct marketing consulting. Darlene was noncommittal about her feelings. Actually I think everyone was glad we

41

don't have the every-six-weeks' deadline hanging over our heads anymore. The fact is, I am the gladdest of all.

April 15: Money. I think it is going to be a lifetime problem. Our accountant brought me all of our tax forms to sign. We don't owe anything, but how do we stay on top of all this? And why did it take her so long to fill everything out and get us the reports we so desperately need? I'm not sure when I can pay her bill, either. Now Pat and I have to start using these financial-report spreadsheets and tracking our own records. No one outside will care as much as we do about the business.

April 17: Had lunch with Ellice J., the superstar saleswoman, again. She told me that you have to have financial goals. That you have to know what you want and work to achieve it. She said that this month she wants to hit her sales goals so that she can buy a JennAir stove for her kitchen. That's how she became such a successful salesperson. I really don't have goals. I work hard every day, and I have monthly sales goals I'd like to hit. But if I don't hit them, I don't worry about it. Mostly I just go on working hard from week to week, making sure that my customers are happy and

---

LESSONS LEARNED

#12: Where Should I Spend My Time? In the Office or Out Meeting With Clients?

There was never an easy answer to this question. I was either in the office doing the work and helping with the bookkeeping, in the office making phone calls to customers, or out trying to get more business. I was also learning how to do both sales and operations.

When I finally hired people to replace me in sales and operations, I had a much better feel for what they needed to do, and that made it easier for me to supervise them. So, the answer for the early years was just to be willing to work lots of hours without feeling sorry for myself. No time for pity, actually. I was learning, and that was fascinating to me.

---

putting out fires the rest of the time. So what am I really doing all this for?

Bill never talks about goals. He wouldn't want to have this conversation. What do I really want?

I want to build something (the company).
I want to be comfortable.
I want money in the bank.
I want a mortgage I can afford.
I would love a tiny cottage in the woods for weekends.
I want employees who know what they are doing.
I want to have the freedom to take some time off now and
    then.
I want to have a family.

I can hear Ellice telling me that isn't enough. That you have to be concrete, attach dollar figures to everything.

On the radio the other day, the announcer said that you have to give yourself permission to do whatever you want. That you

---

LESSONS LEARNED

#13: Finding Mentors and Advisors

Though I was very careful to present a confident front, I was continually wondering how more successful people were doing business. It took me almost eight years to learn to start asking questions out loud. I just met a woman recently who told me that Ellice J. was instrumental in teaching her about sales in her business too. This woman owned a basket company, and Ellice asked her if she had started calling on the largest companies in the city yet (I swear Ellice was born with that kind of confidence). The basket-company owner admitted she hadn't. "Well, you have to go to the top. That's where the big business is. Those people need your services. How will they know you are out there if you don't call on them?" Robin said it changed her business. The very next week she started calling on big corporations, and her sales jumped.

choose the rules you live by. You give yourself what you deserve. Maybe I think I deserve this chaos I am so firmly standing in.

April 18: I met Charlie F., the superstar insurance agent's boss. He is 43 years old and has been an insurance salesman for 20 years. He has built the agency up to 20 agents and has offices in one of the nicest buildings in the city. He is a success and he carries himself as if he knows it.

He is considering hiring us for a telemarketing consulting project. We meet to talk about how I can help support his sales-people with more leads for new business. He tells me that his job is to give his agents a work climate in which they can be successful. Do I create a climate where my salespeople can succeed? What would Dar and Maggi have to do to earn $100,000 per year apiece? They must close on one piece of business per day worth $5,000. Five sales per week? I'm not sure that is even realistic. They would each need a sales assistant to help them stay on top of their leads and prospects. They would have to learn to assess their client's needs and what questions to ask.

April 23: I'm going to go down in history as the world's greatest optimist. From one day to the next I am scheming, planning, burn-ing huge amounts of energy to arrange a carefully constructed plan. Then I go into the office and the plan goes out the window, because I get pulled into the demands of the day: client calls, writ-ing copy, helping to produce work. I cannot ever work my plans as thoroughly as I should.

April 28: Moved into the house on Saturday. We let the sellers live there an extra four months until their house was ready to move into. No time to think about houses and decorating. Just not impor-tant right now.

April 30: I hired Mike J. as a production coordinator who is also a graphic artist. He will replace both Carol M. and Eileen. He has eight years of design and production experience. He met with Liza's approval and will start in a few weeks. Bill told me about him (he did some work for Bill's office). Liza needed too big a salary. I can't believe what they are paying her at D——. Once Mike starts, I'll have some breathing room to help Dar and Maggi. . . .

LESSONS LEARNED

#14: Teaching Your Employees to Be Self-Reliant

I just learned recently that an important character trait small-business employees need is the ability to work well in an unstructured environment. Looking back, I don't think any of my original employees (except for Darlene and me) possessed that trait. It is actually a trait you can test someone for.

But my employees became self-reliant at first because they had no choice. I was never there, and when I was there I was on the phone. Gradually, I learned through weekly meetings, quarterly meetings, and annual meetings that they needed to hear what I was thinking. It was there that I let them know the big picture. Once I began to share where I wanted us to head, my staff seemed to bend over backwards trying to help me get there.

May 6: Mike starts tomorrow. Will he last forever? I'm so tired of this turnover.

May 7: Met with Charlie F. again. This guy has piqued my curiosity. He believes in systems. He is the picture of self-discipline and success. As I ask questions, he talks and talks, coaching me, telling me his theories. He believes that to find good employees, you have to screen very, very carefully. He believes that good salespeople and customer-service people are the key to a successful service business. He devised a 48-question survey to help him identify the characteristics he thinks are important in a good salesperson, as well as using a personality test. I don't have the nerve to ask him for it. He has developed a structured trial period, good training, and a supervisory staff.

May 11: This has been a big week. Ever since I met Ellice and Phil, I can understand how a person can earn $100,000 a year. But it is not by working on $350 projects the way we did when I started the business. It seems almost coincidence, but since I met Ellice and Phil we are being asked to make bigger proposals. Mostly on the telemarketing side, which I don't enjoy as much as direct mail. But

I made a $75,000 proposal to P——. I made a major presentation worth $60,000 to S——. I made a long-term telemarketing and direct mail proposal to W—— worth $100,000. Finally, I met with Charlie F. and he said if we did well with his project, he'd introduce us to every one of his counterparts across the United States. These are exciting times.

May 12: We got the S—— contract on the first appointment. My friend works there. This is our largest contract to date (worth about $30,000 per year for two years). We will design, print, and mail a quarterly newsletter for them. I also think our being chosen was based on the quality of Mike's previous work as an artist and the strength of Ellen's past design work. It is not direct mail in the true sense. But it's work for the business, and it is a client who can work directly with Mike, which means fewer details for me for a change. He started on May 8, and he will take over this account. This is what I've wanted: freedom to go out and get business, knowing I have someone inside who can handle it when I drop it at the front

---

LESSONS LEARNED

#15: Thinking Bigger

After about eight years in the business, I finally talked to enough people who were successful to see that they were calling on a very carefully selected group of prospective customers and expecting a fairly large average sale, or expecting enough long-term revenue to justify their sales efforts. While they were selling $5,000, $10,000, $30,0000 accounts, I was selling $500 projects that sometimes required the same amount of work! But because I was working with tiny companies for consulting and special projects, they could only afford tiny mailings, small marketing contracts.

    Once I finally saw that larger, national companies needed my services, I gradually began to gain the courage to call on them. This was a turning point in my business. Once I felt confident selling our service to larger companies and bundling our services into larger packages, we finally began to make money.

door. No real time to train him, but he seems very comfortable and knows exactly what to do. Eileen and Carol can answer his questions.

May 13: Dad called. Mad at me for sending Eileen home. Told me I should have paid her better because she is my sister. I love her dearly, but she had just graduated from school and had no work experience. I can't pay her more just because she's family. Dad just wants to protect his younger daughter.

May 14: No fun being married to Anita. Vacation in Cape May coming up. Time to slow down. Eileen and Carol leaving in two weeks.

May 15: Two weeks in the new house and haven't done a thing. Too busy at work. I promise Bill I'll be home by 6:30 and I don't pull out the paperwork from my briefcase until after 10:30, when he goes to bed.

May 19: I asked Pat to take our canceled checks and invoices from the last year and post the numbers on job cost sheets, as the two guys recommended in that seminar. This way I can see how profitable each job is. It took her a month to do, and we finally looked at them together on Saturday. I am sick. We aren't making money. It took several days for that terrorizing fact to sink in. But I can't avoid it any longer. The fear of not being able to pay my bills is enormous.

1. I'm going to teach Mike how to calculate an accurate price and tell him that all prices must allow for gross margins and a 10 percent commission.
2. We must tell clients to pay us separately for postage and printing, since these expenses just inflate our sales and fool me into thinking we have more income than we really do.
3. We must set policy and write clear, detailed contracts on how we receive things from clients. If we don't get what we need and it takes more time on our end, we have to charge for it (this is where we lose most of our money).
4. If we can't control costs, we might as well not be in business.

Starting tomorrow, we are a new company. We can never let these costs get away from us again. Pat is going to keep these job cost sheets updated every day by hand. It is more work, but we need to have it done.

May 21: I've been rereading my journals. I realize that I make a lot of commitments to change on paper, but it takes a lot longer to follow through. Especially when it comes to employee problems. Why? Confronting people is hard for me. These people count on me to have all the answers. If I believe in them enough to hire them, then I must have a plan and know what to do next. But I really don't know what I am doing a lot of the time.

May 24: Before we drive to New Jersey for vacation, I ask Bill to take a detour so that we can see V——, a pizza shop one hour out of our way. The owner is a friend of Darlene's cousin who wanted to do a direct mail program. We sit for 45 minutes waiting for him to meet with me. It is lunchtime, and he is exceptionally busy. Bill is furious. I am embarrassed, realizing that I have killed almost three hours, including travel time, for a $400 sale. Worst of all, he tells us when he sits down that he doesn't think he can afford to pay our bill with one check. Can he spread payments over three months? We are here, I have the artwork done. "Sure," I say. He sends us to New Jersey with a free pizza and sodas. I want to own a serious business, but I'll still take any business that comes my way. Free pizza and all. We laugh about it as we finally start our vacation.

May 25: We're staying at a bed and breakfast in Cape May, New Jersey. Whether we like them or not, we have to interact with eight other couples over a five-day weekend. I have been realizing since I started the business how introverted I am. I find the whole experience a little strange. Bill, on the other hand, has camped out on the front porch with a beer for the last two days and can tell me the life story of everyone in the house. He and Darlene are alike in that way. They love being around people. I'd rather write in my journal or work on a project.

I did enjoy sitting with Nancy R., the owner of the B and B. We begin to share marketing and business-owner stories. I feel I have found a club member. Nancy is struggling to keep this place going.

She also hates dealing with payroll, payroll taxes, and accounting. I am not the only one!

When I go back, Carol and Eileen are gone. Mike is there running inside operations. Darlene and I are back to selling a refined set of services full-time. In a way, it's like a new company. I feel the business keeps going forward a little and then backwards a lot. Costwise, I'm paying Mike almost exactly what I was paying Carol and Eileen combined. It's time to see if paying for experience is worth it.

June 10: Sat down with Maggi to tell her she needed to start selling on her own without me. We ended up yelling at each other. I cannot seem to communicate my point well enough. I want to tell her I think she is wonderful and ambitious, but that it takes more than that to get contracts. In almost a year, she has not brought in a single account without my help. She left the office very angry and upset.

June 16: Maggi resigned. It is so hard not to take this all personally, so hard to be objective. I feel as though I tried to get her to do what I needed and she could not do it. Now she is angry and hurt. I did not get into business to affect people's lives like this.

June 18: Meeting with Charlie F. I feel so young and inexperienced compared to him. But I'm confident about what we do. When I talk about our work, I'm comfortable. We're going to set up a telemarketing operation inside his office. I will hire the people, but they will report to his salespeople. This stuff, telemarketing and direct mail, is easy to talk about. I know what I know. But managing employees . . . building a company . . . those are still uncomfortable subjects for me.

I do not tell him that we are building an incredible backlog of employee tax withholdings. We are slowly working it off, but it is now the biggest number we owe. It must be over $5,000 by now. I do not even know exactly because I do not understand how to calculate it. But our accountant has it figured out. She also recommended we contact a payroll service called Paychex. They could handle all the paychecks and calculate what we owe in taxes for every pay period.

LESSONS LEARNED

#16: In Praise of Payroll Services

The need to understand tax withholdings in addition to all the other stuff we have to learn as business owners makes using a payroll service an easy decision. I wish someone had told me about it when I started the business. The payroll service can even file all the withholdings for you, so that the details of payroll taxes are kept behind a curtain. You as owner just have to make sure enough money is there in the checking account to cover the payroll and employer liabilities.

June 22: Kate Smith died. She was known for a lot of things, but mostly for singing "God Bless America." Imagine being so strongly identified with one song that everyone knows you that way. Some celebrities do that. Some corporations do it. We don't do that. We do a little bit of everything.

While I am worrying about the business, Darlene's dad is dying and Pat's mother is very ill. The world keeps making rotations, and everyone puts one foot in front of the other no matter what.

Without the extra sales staff and the cancellation of "Neighborhood," we are actually doing okay. Four of our bigger clients from "Neighborhood" agreed to continue their mailings. We are billing $5,000 less without "Neighborhood" every month. But our expenses from "Neighborhood" were about $5,000 per edition. Bills are getting paid. I'm going to start getting a paycheck through this payroll service. It is really a draw, but it will come to me every two weeks just like everyone else: $200 every two weeks.

The kind of business we are getting now is a little different. Larger jobs, larger companies. The original idea of helping tiny businesses just doesn't work.

June 25: I feel like a jerk because I have to talk to Darlene while she is being turned inside out by her Dad. But I need for her to keep helping with the business, and it has been almost 10 weeks since she has been doing anything while her Dad is so sick. Yet the drain on our payroll is tough.

July 3: Dar's dad died on Thursday.

July 7: Pat's mother died. Will the office ever be normal again?

July 8: Met with Mike and Darlene. There is some conflict between them, but I can't seem to figure out why. Told them I thought if they worked together they could bring in a million dollars per year. But I need Darlene to do the sales and Mike to produce the work. They said they are ready. We've agreed to meet quarterly to review goals. Right now our monthly gross billings have dropped to $12,000–15,000 per month, mostly from direct mail projects.

July 13: Am still faced with a mountain of debt—more than $20,000. About half of it is in credit cards. I have to find ways to reduce expenses. I hired a group of women (Darlene's neighbor, Karen R., and her friends) to help us with mailings instead of using a mail service. My goal was to reduce expenses, but some of these women are slow, and our costs for their services keep escalating. But Karen is definitely the fastest of all the workers. Maybe if I ask her to not hire the slower women, we will spend less and produce the same results. Also, I need to get Pat to make regular phone calls to collect invoices older than 30 days. Keep plugging. I heard on the radio that the guy who invented Coca Cola only sold 400 cases in his first year.

It is also getting a little easier at work, thanks to Mike handling production, and Karen handling the mailings, and Darlene being a little more experienced.

July 20: On the way back from a sailing weekend with friends, we talked about pets we have loved. By the time we got home early Sunday afternoon, Bill and I had talked ourselves right into adopting a pet. At 4:30 we came home with two six-month-old puppies from the animal shelter.

July 21: With Maggi gone, we are back to Darlene being the only full-time person prospecting for new business, while I am spending 20 percent of my time on new business and the rest working with existing customers. The project with Charlie F.'s agents has been frustrating. His salespeople all have secretaries, and I was hired to teach the secretaries how to do telemarketing. Mostly, they hate doing it, and some of the salespeople are young, inexperienced managers. Phil B. and some of the others don't praise their employees or supervise them closely enough. Some consulting projects are more satisfying than others. This one is definitely not making me feel good. But some of the women are getting good results, so the salespeople are happy.

August 3: I finally feel excited about the business. I can see clearly how we are different from our competitors. Mike's design and production work makes our services even easier to sell. No one in town seems to have my depth of telemarketing experience. But my problem is I can't seem to pass that enthusiasm onto Darlene. She and I have worked together through tremendous ups and downs, and we've seen a lot of people come and go as I learned what it is I was doing. Now that I finally feel confident, I can't seem to keep Dar on the same page. I know she's still disconnected because of her dad. Have I lost her?

August 12: Dar asked if we could talk. She is disappointed that she still isn't making money, and she is also disappointed in me (though she doesn't say that). When she left W—— to join me, I hadn't really made many mistakes yet. Of course not, with all the resources of W——, and the systems and the staff and the budget of W——, behind me. But out here, it is totally different.

So Dar is going to start looking for firmer ground. I guess I don't blame her. I want us to be friends, but right now I just have to help her find a job with a bigger, more stable company.

August 13: Met with Phil B. regarding his project. He makes six figures and has a country-club bill bigger than what I earned last month. But he is also driven. In the office at 6:30 A.M., four to five appointments per day, five days per week. Very disciplined. Does everything he is supposed to. No excuses. Everything else besides work is secondary. Can I live that way? Totally devoted and focused on work and nothing else? For now, yes. But forever? I don't think so.

September 21: Dad and Lucy got married today. Gorgeous wedding. I pretended to be just a girl at the wedding. Eileen and I did not talk about the business. It is their day.

September 23: Money obsessions again. I used to just want $10,000 in a savings account at the bank. I said if I had that I'd be happy. Then I got into this business and started meeting people whom I considered successful, and now I can't even come up with an amount in a savings account that would make me happy. I stood in line at the bank to deposit $3,000. The girl in front of me was depositing less than $300. But I felt poor. We live in a comfortable house in a safe neighborhood, have two cars that start every morning, have a great marriage, travel somewhere on vacation at least twice a year, have good friends . . . and yet, I'm depressed about money most of the time. What is my problem?

LESSONS LEARNED

#17: Rising Above the Basic Needs for Money

This is an issue for women, mostly. We are not used to thinking about generating any more money for ourselves than we need to get by. Somehow I had to learn that it was okay to want to make more than my parents made, more than my friends, more than the sum of our monthly expenses. I had to think about making enough to sock money away, enough to build a pension fund, enough to repay myself for all the income I lost from stepping off the corporate track. Once I set my sights on growing the business large enough to support a well-paid staff, pension and health benefits, enough money in reserves for slow times, and a paycheck I could be proud of, then the numeric goals changed. It was easier to set my sites on building a company that did $1 million, $5 million, $10 million in gross annual sales. I could also see more clearly how I could reward myself and my employees for hitting those goals.

October 5: Got back from vacation at Deep Creek. Disastrous. Bill hurt his back on the second day, the dogs barked at every sound all night long, and it rained for six days in a row. I have watched every movie the rental place had on their racks. Is this punishment for not bringing my briefcase?

October 7: The consulting project I had with Charlie F. is going terribly. They don't follow the instructions I give them. They are not treating the telemarketers I hired with any respect. This work is frustrating. Charlie has also asked that I set up the contract so that each of the 10 salespeople in the program pays one-tenth of my contract. Charlie is no longer the client. He doesn't have the expense on his books. I have 10 more clients, and I'm right back to having tiny contracts again. This isn't what I had in mind.

October 15: Saw Ellen M. and Jan G. over lunch last week. I have known both women as friends for years. Both accused me of the same thing: They talk about their problems, their needs, their fears, and I just listen. When it comes to my turn, I ask for the check. They complain because I don't talk about my own problems. I am so in the habit of keeping everything to myself or telling Bill (edited versions of my work life) that I have nothing to say to them. Neither of them owns a business. How can they possibly help me? The easiest outsider to talk to lately has been Liza B. She is a vendor and a friend who understands our industry very well, and she knows the company and the players. She's the one who has been listening to my problems lately. And I hate complaining. So by the time I sit down with good friends, I'm out of steam.

October 16: Mike wants us to invest $3,500 in a camera and some equipment to help him generate artwork in-house rather than use a vendor. But right now we only spend $100 per month for artwork. Doesn't make sense. Am I ready to cut into our already slender margins? I think we should wait until next year and see how things go. Mike is not happy but accepts my decision.

October 24: Got a big direct mail project from R—— through an old neighbor. She and I lived on the same block a few years ago, and we bumped into each other in town. It's amazing, the longer I'm in business the more that seems to happen. I wonder how much busi-

---

LESSONS LEARNED

#18: On the Advantages of Sharing Your Real Fears

I spent most of my time in business pretending that everything was just fine. I didn't want to scare my employees. I would never consider telling my clients what I didn't understand. I didn't think my friends would understand, since none of them owned businesses. No one in my family had their own business during my early years. So who was there to tell?

Now I do ask a lot more questions and am freer to admit what I don't know. But it has been like exercising a muscle. At first it was painful. As I did it more frequently, it got more comfortable. And finally, releasing my fears and asking for advice actually made me stronger. I learned faster.

---

ness we will have in 20 years of seeing the same people and building a network?

Actually, I still feel overworked and underpaid. And I want the quality of our work to be better. (Mike needs to keep working on details.) I still feel I'm involved with every decision at work. But with three or four jobs coming in every week, if I stopped and met with him every time there'd be no time to go out and sell. I just have to keep checking work before it goes out the door and answer questions from the road. I need to work even more overtime and ask everyone else to do the same.

October 29: Nothing will be the same again. Bill's mom is very sick. She is also the one person who listens to all my problems without judging me. She couldn't care less if I owned this business or worked as a check-out clerk in the mall. There are some problems I can't fix no matter how much I try. I don't pray very much, but I will try.

November 5: Problems again. Arms of a bear around my stomach. Problems with R—— job (Mike ordered final printed copies without getting the client's approval and they wanted to make last-minute changes); also problems with W—— job, problems with A—— job, problems with D——. Mike is angry and barely civil to

customers. Bill's birthday is in two days, and I have no money to buy
him a present. And the mortgage and car payments are overdue.

November 7: Took Bill out to dinner and bought him a new lens for
his camera. Charged it. He asks when we are going to get together
with friends and make plans for Christmas. I don't want to see anyone. I don't want anyone to ask me about the business. I don't want
to listen to their problems, and I don't want to tell them mine. I
want to go to work, come home, and crawl into bed.

November 9: I realize that these puppies require a routine that
never existed for me before. I usually hate doing the same thing
twice in a row. I often take a different route back from an appointment from the one I took getting there. But these pups hate changes
in the routine. They get great comfort from being let out at the same
times every day, fed at the same times, exercised at the same times.
They depend on us totally for their comfort, so being a little consistent is the least we can do for them.

November 10: Typical Monday. Pat tells me the typewriter is bro-
ken and it will take two weeks and $180 to fix. We have to buy a
new one, which will cost $350. Then in the mail I get a notice that
we owe $300 in back taxes (an error). Then I have a production
meeting with Mike, and we talk about a job that has been in his
hands for two weeks, and he still is confused about certain details,
and the client needed it yesterday. And then before the end of the
day the phone rings and it is a company asking us to come in and
make a major presentation. I leave work on a high. No wonder I get
chest pains.

November 15: More problems with a new client. They found us
through the Yellow Pages. Emergency job that must be done before
Thanksgiving. When I took the project, I thought a regular vendor
could do it for us. But now that the job is in, our vendor says she is
shutting down for the week before Thanksgiving and can't take the
job. I can't believe it! How can someone promise to do something
and then back out without even an apology? We never say no. We
always say "no problem" and then figure out a way. So that's
where we are with this. I am determined to meet the deadline, and
we will have to find another vendor.

LESSONS LEARNED

#19: Acting Like a Big Company Even When You Are Small

I always felt, even when I was working out of my bedroom, that we had to act serious, even if we were tiny. That meant answering the phones 24 hours per day (using an answering machine when I wasn't there). It meant delivering consistent services in a professional manner (even if the reality was that the owner was working like a lunatic and asking family members to do the same thing). It meant formally prepared proposals, solid marketing materials, and backup vendors who could provide adjunct services so that we never had to turn down work.

November 16: Found another vendor. It's a small company owned by a couple who've agreed to rent us their equipment on short notice. But they are not sure they have the staff to run it for all the hours we need to get the job done on time. I offer to provide them with people who will go to their office to run the equipment. We just don't have the computers and high-speed printers to do the whole project.

November 19: Nightmare job. After three days and all-nighters, we finally get the entire job in the mail—but not without two equipment failures and two last-minute employee replacements. Darlene's two sons helped after school. Even Bill came down and worked with me last night until 4 A.M. and then went to work this morning. I vowed that since Plan A didn't work, we would follow Plan B. Then as things happened I just kept saying no problem, go to Plan C, Plan D, Plan E. . . . This morning as I drove the job to the post office I counted. We got to Plan M. I feel lucky to have such wonderful support from everyone. But I am definitely not in the holiday spirit.

November 29: Just finished another direct mail job that involved using this couple and their office equipment. It's time to consider buying our own equipment. It will cost $11,600. But these two jobs brought in more than $20,000.

December 7: I read in a magazine that at the end of the year you should make a list of your goals and put them in an envelope, to be opened in five years. So what goals would I put into my envelope?

1. My business will generate $200,000 per year.
2. We will have a growing staff, adequate equipment to do our work, and a nice office to work in.
3. Our house will be close to paid for, and we will have two kids.
4. My dogs will sit and heel on command from across a crowded room.
5. I'll have a 24 handicap in golf.
6. All my friends and family will be happy and healthy, including Bill's mom.

December 8: Bill's mom called. Her house is two blocks from our new house, and she spends lots of time sitting by the window now. Called to say she could see our Christmas lights from her kitchen. I switched them on and off for her to be sure they were our lights she saw. So how can any other goal be more important than number 6?

December 20: Saturday afternoon. Bad week. Feel sick to my stomach, lethargic, unable to move, read, write. Settled in five feet from the television, wrapped in a comforter with the dogs sleeping on my legs. I know I have friends who don't care how much money I make. I know I have an understanding husband who feels the same way. But I still seem to struggle over money. We quote a maximum price tag on a job and then discover in the middle of it that there is more involved. So we keep our mouths shut, do the job anyway, and eat the extra expense. And then here I sit. I just to have to learn to stop doing some things.

1. Is it time to hire a better salesperson than Darlene? Someone who is capable of bringing in more sales?
2. Is it time to stop doing everything in-house? If we hired a mailing company again to stuff and seal direct mailings

for a flat fee, we could get their quote, mark it up, and be guaranteed to make a profit. Instead, when Karen does the mailings, sometimes she does them in less than the time budgeted, but most of the time not.

3. It is time to raise our minimum job price tag. We simply cannot take in a job or new customer worth less than $1,000 per year.

4. We have to do a better job collecting our overdue accounts. People owe us money, but Pat is afraid to call them. Yet she hates it when one of our vendors calls us.

December 23: Today the business seems clearer in my mind. I understand what I enjoy about it. I love the freedom of owning my own business. I love meeting people and discussing ideas and then translating those ideas into services. I love creating something from nothing. I love helping clients focus on their problems and then working out solutions. I love the marketing tools I know best: direct mail and telemarketing. They are easy to use, explain, justify. I love being able to jump in my car and go on an appointment, or sit at my desk and write, or push everything aside and make phone calls. I love being the one in charge of my own future.

Next year we will continue to market our design, direct mail, mailing services, telemarketing consulting, and marketing consulting services.

January 3: Project with Charlie F., to conduct the telemarketing training, is over. We met for the last time and reviewed the project. I learned that all agents across the country ask their salespeople to pay all overhead costs, including marketing programs like mine. So unless I want to deal directly with salespeople, which creates all kinds of billing and collections problems (three of his agents have still not paid me), I don't want Charlie to refer me to his counterparts across the country. We shake hands. I'm glad I met him.

January 4: Asked Bill to help me take photographs for the L—— brochure. Since we had been talking about his joining the company some day, I thought it would work out. Plus he is a great photographer that I can get for free. (Okay, I promised to buy him a new pair of running shoes.) But it turned out horribly. His attitude is: Take the picture, develop the film, and see what happens. But we have a deadline. These pictures must be perfect. If they aren't wonderful, I can't meet the deadline, and that will be a reflection on the business.

January 7: Dinner with Ellice J. again. We agreed to get together in the evenings to swap trade secrets. I would teach her how to do more effective telemarketing; she would teach me how to sell. This was our first session. I like to think I'm doing most things right. But she pointed out some ways I could improve.

1. She reminded me that I didn't write enough handwritten notes.
2. She reminded me that I needed to be a better, more understanding coach to Darlene.
3. She taught me better questions to ask in meetings, such as, "What would it take for us to work together?" Love that one. She also made me realize that she takes her work more seriously than I take this business. If I had been really serious, I'd have brought in a million dollars in business, as she did last year.

January 8: I read an article in *Venture* magazine about a business that failed. The postmortem was grim. They regretted a lot of moves they made. They only lasted five months and lost $27,000. I've been in business for two-and-a-half years and have invested more than $27,000. If I closed my doors today, you could write the same story about me. I just would have suffered longer.

January 20: This morning I asked Dar to meet me in the office at 8:30. There had been a major problem with a job we did for Dwight F. His mailing went out incorrectly after he specifically asked for certain letters to go with certain labels. Dar brought in the job and didn't provide Mike and Karen with the proper details. Now his customers are calling him to complain. It is a major problem. We will have to eat the cost of redoing the entire mailing. If she had given me proper instructions, none of this would have happened. I can't keep going on this way. Anyway, when she came into the meeting, she gave me her letter of resignation. I felt horrible and relieved. Why did I hire a friend?

January 21: Darlene is gone. I am sick. I still can't believe it. In some ways, I'm angry with myself and with her. Because of her, we took a detour with the company and started offering a product that required staff and vendors and an office. And here I sit now with this company and these employees and this office. And she is gone. Is this what I really set out to do? What happened to being free and independent?

January 26: In looking back, I think blaming the detour on Darlene is a little lame. I finally am getting the chance to decide what I really want to do in business.

February 28: Hired Colleen R., the daughter of a client, to help me in the office as my assistant. Although she worked for her dad when she got out of school, this is her first real job. We finally bought a computer, and she is the most dexterous of us on it—she's the youngest in the office and learned to use computers in school. Pat is deathly afraid of the machines. It will be easier and cheaper with Colleen than hiring and training a full-time salesperson. That way I can go out and sell and meet with clients and she can handle inquiries coming into the office. No risk this way. I'm the only one selling and working with clients; everyone else is support staff. Simple.

March 5: Met Tom F. He is the head of marketing at Q—— and has offered us a great shot at a telemarketing project. Found us through the Yellow Pages. This will be different from the project with Charlie F. If I provide the callers, they can work out of his offices. But they will be my employees; he can't tell them what to do. And after the project is over in eight weeks, I'm free to reassign them, lay them off, or do whatever I choose. He wants me to supervise them, monitor them, and make sure they meet his objectives.

I love this idea. What I hated about telemarketing consulting was the way my clients treated the people I hired and trained. This way, they can be my employees. Tom's the most experienced telemarketing person I've met in this city. Says he wants to have 20,000 businesses called in the next six weeks. He also asked a ton of questions about the business.

I'm going to do it. And then I'm going to go out and sell the services of these callers to other companies, to start again when this job is over. The project is worth about $60,000 if we get it.

LESSONS LEARNED

#20: Developing Products That Are Project-Related vs. Ones That Generate Recurring Revenue

The one aspect of our business that kept us very weak was that we lived from project to project. I felt the downside of that often: Lack of business meant laying off good people. It meant more pressure to sell the next project. It meant no long-term relationships with companies, where you served them for years and years.

Now I look at every new client and try to figure out how I can turn this project into one that renews annually. Had I done that from the beginning, we would have struggled less, I think.

March 8: We got it. We start immediately.

March 18: Just when I have decided to downsize, simplify, and rethink my direction, a huge opportunity like the Q—— project looms in front of me, too big to ignore. Maybe it is impossible to really plan in business. Maybe organic growth is the best. This project was a good decision. It is going very well, and I already have a few people considering using us for telemarketing when this project is over.

LESSONS LEARNED

#21: How to Respond When the Client Buys You Lunch and Then Asks You for a Job

Smile sweetly, throw half the check on the table, and tell them you absolutely never hire clients. It is a policy recommended to you by the corporate board of directors. (Okay, so you are the sole shareholder; that's irrelevant.) You can't win with this one.

March 20: It's almost exactly two months since Darlene left. I have no excuses now. I have to be the one to build this company. No waiting for Darlene's ideas about "Neighborhood." No waiting for her to find someone who wants to talk to me.

March 30: Tom. F. from Q—— (the big client) bought me lunch today and told me confidentially that he wants to be a partner. And that his contract could be the first account in our new company. I don't want a partner, yet I'm not sure how to respond, since he is a client.

April 1: Today is our third birthday! Happy birthday to me! Three whole years as the head of Direct Response Marketing. I can't believe it.

End of Year Three

Year Four

Executive Summary

Type of work:	Direct mail services, design, telemarketing consulting, mailing-list services, and trying telemarketing production
Business location:	500 square feet in suburban hotel
Number of employees:	5 (mostly part-time)
Sources of new business:	Referrals, word of mouth, newsletter, attendance at professional and chamber meetings
Investment capital:	Personal credit cards
Average monthly sales:	$20,000
Average sale:	$1,000
Annual revenue:	Approx. $240,000
Greatest challenge:	Without Darlene and "Welcome to the Neighborhood," I was totally alone and selling myself. Very scary.
Comments:	Darlene resigned. Abandoned "Welcome to the Neighborhood" (the new-resident mailing program that Darlene and I developed and produced together), concentrated on providing direct mail services and consulting to key accounts, paid attention to improving my own sales ability.

April 12: It's been 12 weeks since Darlene left. I'm still the only one selling. Mike J. and Colleen are helping me service our accounts, and I hired Fran M. to manage the telemarketing group. Pat is qui-

etly doing my typing, sending invoices, writing checks, keeping manual financial records, and rolling her eyes every time I tell her of some new decision of mine. She's very practical and can't understand why we aren't still in the back bedroom of the apartment doing consulting. We offer so many services that when I write the newsletter I have to devote every article to a different service area. We might have to print a larger newsletter with this issue. I also find it hard to explain to people what we do. Usually, I'll ask them what they do. Then I explain the services I think they will probably need.

I miss Darlene. But I feel good that she is not here. She was so unhappy, and I felt responsible for that.

Also I want to work with Mike, to teach him to assess the difference between good and bad work. I looked at the W——job and could see instantly what was wrong. He didn't see it. He says I'm being picky. Is it me, or is it him?

I can only admit it here that I'm wavering on this idea of maintaining our own telemarketing department. All these extra people to worry about puts me in the lying-in-bed-calculating-payroll game again. I did rent the room next to ours and installed eight more phone lines. Fran and "the girls," as she calls them, will be moving back into our offices next week. But I'm scared to death.

We have two telemarketing projects starting next week. In the meantime, all the callers are going to help me prospect for new business.

Maybe I should save my money, wait until the fall, and hire a salesperson to help me sell direct mail services instead. I can just thank everyone for helping with the Q—— project and move back to what I was doing before.

We are at a crossroads. I'm taking the company in a new direction. Darlene is gone. I am still not doing what I started out wanting to do: consulting. Now I own a direct mail and telemarketing service bureau instead of a quiet little consulting firm. I'm not sure where I'm headed.

May 11: Vacation journal. Two weeks in Myrtle Beach with Bill. Vacation started badly. The day I left we were expecting a check from Q—— that would have covered payroll. It didn't come. I called Pat from the road, and she told me no checks came in. I asked her to call Q——and said I would call her back. When I did, she said that the check would not be issued for another week. From a pay phone in Virginia, I called my mutual fund and had the $4,000 for payroll transferred from my fund into the company checking account. But it wouldn't happen till the following Monday. No one was going to get paid on payday, and Pat was going to have to explain it.

May 14: I call the office again. Everyone got their checks. They said they understood. Pat is shaken but okay. This vacation will not be fun. I screw up our bank account too much. Because I hate doing the accounting, I always leave it till last. It's time to share the hard cold fact with Pat (she probably knows it anyway) that I can't do this, and ask her to help me. I can give her a raise or take away some of her other responsibilities so she'll have the time for it. Maybe Colleen can help answer the phones so that Pat doesn't have to and can concentrate on our financial work.

We need more sales. I can't do this by myself. And what really drives me batty is the debt. Just before I left W ——, I had all our bills paid, money in the bank, and zero debt. It felt like total free-

---

LESSONS LEARNED

#22: On Making Money

Up to this point, my two critical mistakes were (1) not focusing on a single service and (2) not creating a systematic way of selling that service. When I had Darlene, she was attempting to sell systematically. We had a service ("Neighborhood"). But I didn't focus on it. I was all over the playing field instead.

I believe now that had I thrown all of my energy, commitment, and resources into that single service, and figured out systematically how to bring in new advertisers for it, we could have made a very successful business out of that idea alone.

My problem was, the idea didn't interest me as much as it interested Darlene. I needed to be emotionally committed early on, and I was not.

---

dom. I don't want to live for paying bills. I have wiped out our two savings accounts.

May 18: Vacations are always a time when I get geographic distance from this business that consumes me. From a distance, it still looks as if I can't decide what business we are in. I thought that hiring Mike would be my answer for solving operations problems. Instead, he causes more problems. I thought without Darlene I would be free to sell the services I enjoyed working with (direct mail, marketing consulting). Instead I find myself reverting to my old fear of cold calling. I hide out in the office fixing operations problems in between visits with existing clients.

May 19: Still on vacation, and thinking about work. I'm not ready to set up a separate telemarketing company with Tom F. I'm not even comfortable with how he wants to control the company and remain a client. Just doesn't smell right. I don't need to buy Tom's expertise by giving away half of my company, and I don't really want an outside investor telling me what to do. I'll talk to him when I go back home.

May 20: Mike is driving me crazy. Whenever there is a problem, it's never his fault. He thinks our clients are stupid. He talks about them behind their backs if he thinks I'm not listening. Whenever I ask him about a client conversation where he doesn't have an answer, he'll say, "The client didn't tell me." I want him to say, "I forgot to ask that question."

May 26: Most recent job for P—— crashed miserably. This time it was not Mike's fault. I saw it coming and did not do what I needed to stop it. I should have gone to F. (at P——) in the very beginning and told him that we were not equipped to handle the job. But I was determined; I don't like turning work away. I thought we could handle it. And then I just didn't know how to say "enough." Now we've spent $2,000 more than we charged P—— for the job and will do it over anyway. No wonder we're not making any money.

May 29: Told Tom F. that partnering with him to start a telemarketing company wouldn't work. I don't want his investment. I also tell him I feel he is one of the most knowledgeable telemarketing

---

LESSONS LEARNED

**#23: Operations Problems and How to Avoid
Some of Them**

The problem with offering so many services is that I was our only
safety net. I was the only one on staff who knew how to execute all of
our services, so we were only as good as the limits of my knowledge.
Had I outsourced more regularly, limited my range of services, and
hired people with direct experience in this limited range of services,
I would have had fewer problems.

---

people I've met in this city and that I'm flattered he asked me. He
says he understands. [Note: He leaves town four months later.]

June 5: Talked to Liza. She could be joining us as soon as August
15. She will make more than I do and more than anyone else in the
company, but this is the only solution I can think of. She is one of
six salespeople at her company (they are a design and video production company) and regularly brings in $50,000 accounts. Last
year she brought in $300,000 in sales. If all goes well, in a few years
we will talk about partnership.

June 6: Poor Bill. Trouble at home. He doesn't feel well. He says he
wants to get rid of the house and the dogs, buy a travel trailer, and
drive across the country. Here I am waist deep in this business with
no interest at all in traveling or changing anything. But I do see that
unless I figure out a way to keep my work week under 50 hours
and put systems in place to protect our income, then our marriage
will be in trouble too.

July 1: Got the call late at night. Grandma died. She'd been very sick.

July 2: Went home for the funeral. A few family members look at
my little four-cylinder sedan and remind me that if I want to project an executive image I should be driving a nicer car. I am angry
but don't argue. The business can't afford a nicer car. But for a

moment I doubt myself. In a way, the company has caused me to lose my confidence. I have lost my confidence about my ability to hire good employees. I'm praying that Liza is a good decision.

I've lost confidence in my ability to manage money. But I do know with all my heart that keeping expenses down is what is protecting us while I make all of these mistakes. When I think about it, the only time I feel truly confident is when I'm with my customers.

July 5: Bill's mom is sick again. Nothing else seems important.

July 10: Had lunch with Barb M. (it's been more than two years since I've seen her), and we talked about our companies. I tell her we are doing fine. She tells me the same. We don't really admit to anything for two hours and go our separate ways.

July 14: Met with Liza to talk about the business. Realized that we could get rid of everyone else in the company except Liza, Pat, and

---

LESSONS LEARNED

#24: Why I Grew Beyond My Own Capabilities

From the time I started, I was secretly enamored with the idea of creating a company with lots of employees. Early on, I started thinking about delegating and sharing responsibility. My only reference was my previous job, where I ran my department like a little company.

What I had not realized was that I inherited that department from a man in his fifties who had built and run that department for 30 years before me. I really had no clue about how to build something as big as 50 employees.

I entered the business with an incorrect assessment of my skills. Somehow, I stumbled my way through. If I were starting a new business today, I would know with much more clarity what skills I lack and how to look at an employee's previous experience so that I could complement and enhance the services of the company.

I finally realized that I grew beyond my own capabilities because I needed the skills of many people to truly deliver a consistent service over the long term.

me and the business would be great. We could concentrate on design and direct mail, which are Liza's areas of expertise, and drop the headaches of all the telemarketing employees and the payroll. But it is not realistic to think we can just randomly let people go. It isn't right. I persuaded them all to leave other jobs to join me. They deserve a chance. I just have to sell more telemarketing and leave Liza alone to sell the other services.

Started working with a new client, H. Said he wants to try some direct mail. He is a car dealer who has been in business for more than 40 years. He talks with authority; he keeps pictures of all his possessions hanging on his office wall; he listens to no one. Yet he asked for my help with marketing. I gave him my opinion, and he gave me a hundred reasons why it was a bad idea. Then he told me about every great idea he ever had.

At one point he invited his senior salesperson into the office and said, "Tell her what my greatest marketing idea was. . . . " The salesperson just turned to H. as if he had done it a hundred times and asked, "What's the right answer, H.?"

So how did this blustery person become so successful? He is one of the most confident people I've ever met. Will I ever know so much that I don't need to doubt my decisions?

July 19: Q—— project went well, and it's over. Now I've got Fran (the telemarketing manager) and six other callers working from tables in our office. We got the empty office next door for another $100 per month. I found two other companies that want to use our telemarketing staff for a project. Fran has also started helping Pat by making collections calls. Since I hate cold calling, I had the telemarketers help me, but they didn't turn up a whole lot. I didn't train them very well because I was busy. I also started talking to everyone I knew, telling them we were now doing telemarketing from our offices. We got these two accounts through referrals. I find it easiest to sell our services when I can see the results and feel confident that we can actually help someone. With this telemarketing program, I can finally see a marketing service that I feel really excited about.

July 23: Met Darlene last night for dinner. Talked about our days at W——. It was good to see her, but still hard to talk about DRM. We talked around it most of the night.

This is our fourth month in a row of slow sales. I'm the only one selling, and we are starving. I can't see how we can afford Liza, yet I can't see myself doing this alone anymore. And I'm also servicing our current clients and overseeing Mike, Fran, Colleen, Pat, Karen, and all the others. To pay Liza in August, we will need to jump from $12,000 per month in sales to $45,000 per month. Can she bring in the other $33,000 per month? Yes, I'm sure she can.

August 2: Karen R., my direct mail department manager, and her crew are working on the C—— job while Bill and I take a Saturday drive to the country. It is the first time we have had a major job where I am not at work. Karen knows what she's doing. I know they can handle it. I seem to make them nervous when I'm there. They don't want me to help them.

August 8: I didn't talk to anyone about the decision, but I couldn't wait anymore. I called Liza and asked to meet with her yesterday. I offered Liza the job and she accepted. She starts next week. I will tell Pat not to pay me for the next month or two until Liza's sales start coming in.

August 15: Liza is now with us. She's helping in both sales and production and is making more than anyone else, and more than twice as much as I'm making. Pat hesitated when I told her the salary, $36,000, but I assured her it was a good decision. Liza is the first experienced salesperson we've ever had. Her salary is an investment.

August 24: Yesterday Mike resigned. Liza spent the last two weeks scrutinizing everything he did (she had no choice, since her desk was less than five feet from his). She confirmed what I had suspected: He was not being completely truthful with vendors or customers. He was really out of his league. Liza said not to worry; he was hurting more than helping us. But the road ahead is clear. No more jobs mishandled. Liza was able to show me what Mike was doing wrong. Pat is very upset about his leaving. I feel terrible when this happens: Sorry I hired him in the first place, and then sorry I wasn't smart enough to make it work or detect the real problem and fix it.

LESSONS LEARNED

#25: Start-Up Time for a New Salesperson

If Mike hadn't quit, we wouldn't have been able to handle the payroll of both Mike and Liza. I was paying Liza too much money. Pat realized that right away.

It was completely in error to hire Liza with a high guaranteed salary, with the assumption that she would bring in sales to cover her salary in the first month. Today I know that I might pay a salesperson's salary for six months before starting to see a return. So when calculating compensation, I need to be sure I have enough money coming in from existing accounts to cover that salary.

As it turned out, Mike's resignation helped pay for Liza.

August 31: The next four months should be very exciting. No clients blaming Mike for missed details, and no surprise invoices from vendors for services I didn't authorize. Liza and I are going to review our pricing and change policies based on her previous experience. After work starts flowing in, we will find a competent designer who can handle our jobs. Liza is taking responsibility for bringing in $30,000 per month in new business. I will devote the majority of my time to running the office, working on new telemarketing business, and managing the jobs as Liza brings them in.

LESSONS LEARNED

#26: Should I Be in Sales, or Operations?

I should have stayed in sales and hired a really good operations person, or let Liza stay inside the company while I stayed outside selling. I was looking for a magical solution to overcome my fear of cold calling. I thought Liza had that solution.

September 2: If Tom F. thought there was a market for our telemarketing services, then it seemed worth looking into. I spent the summer promoting the service and have found some interest. Can I build us into the finest telemarketing company in the city? I've made a commitment to Liza, though, and her background is in print advertising, direct mail, and video production. Maybe I can concentrate on telemarketing and Liza can concentrate on direct mail.

September 18: Liza and I made a direct mail proposal to P——— yesterday. Worth $120,000. We did a fabulous job: The idea was fantastic, the presentation piece flawless. Liza convinced me to pay an illustrator from her former job to help us by producing a prototype of our idea ($1,000 I don't have). But we don't have a chance in hell of getting it. I made the mistake of going over S.'s head to make the presentation to his boss. It didn't work. We presented to both S. and his boss. S. spent the entire meeting smoking his cigar and staring at the ceiling.

Even though we aren't going to get this, Liza taught me what was involved with a professional six-figure proposal. She acted as if it were a three-figure proposal. And so did the people we were presenting it to. These huge companies are used to huge numbers—they're just black ink on paper. I still treat each proposal as

---

LESSONS LEARNED

#27: The Lesson Liza Taught Me

Liza came from a company that had enough cash flow to spend staff time producing prototypes to take into proposal meetings. I had never spent money getting a new contract. But Liza's company regularly made six-figure proposals and had staff who could produce a prototype. What I've learned about big account sales is that prototypes aren't usually necessary. What is necessary is having the confidence to call on them in the first place. Liza raised my sights. For that I will always be grateful.

though I were presenting to myself and as if when I say yes, I'll be spending my own money.

September 26: Bill's mom was rushed to the hospital. Same problem as before.

September 27: I want to move from our office to something nicer and larger. Our current building is for sale and the rumor is that our offices will be torn down, which explains the lack of maintenance and housekeeping over the last six months. I've been seeing mice in the halls. It's time.

Called Barb M. to see what she thought. She suggested we buy a building as an investment. Her father bought their company's warehouse and office building years ago. But her company is almost 40 years old (third-generation business), so they can probably afford that. I'm not sure we can swing it.

Also talked to Dwight F., still a good friend of Darlene's and still one of our clients. He negotiated a long-term lease for his company in a building near us. His advice was to find an owner who also rents space in the building and negotiate with them directly. Don't deal with agents, he says.

October 2: Since Liza got here in August, we have made more big proposals to large companies than ever before. But nothing is converting into contracts. We're still paying bills with the accounts I brought in before she ever came along.

October 12: Today I found out that a colleague of mine folded up his direct mail agency and went to work for a large ad agency. I envied him his business, his nice office, and his vision to be the best in the field. In a way he was a competitor, and in a way he was a role model. I wanted to have a business just like his. But his biggest client merged with another company. He had the same problem as Bill K., our first typesetting vendor. Bill K. also has one major client who pays all the bills. Is this a common business practice? Live off of one big client and go out of business when the client moves on? Maybe figuring out a system for getting lots of little clients does have value. And now, slowly, it's getting a little easier for me. I actually have been taking more weekends off to spend with Bill.

LESSONS LEARNED

#28: The Seduction of the Mega-Account

In all my years in business, I have not met an owner or a salesperson who is not seduced by the mega-account. Now I feel that it is necessary to go after them regularly to really build a business. But at the same time, it's essential to keep looking for customers at the smaller end and keep them happy as well. One of my present board members feels that no account should be worth more than 15 percent of gross sales. I think you could go up to 25 percent without being crippled if their business dried up. As our business grows, I believe my role is to continue looking for mega-accounts while my sales force goes after the smaller business. In fact, when I get sales reports from the sales team, I do not allow them to project a potential account as worth any more than $50,000 (when reporting on outstanding proposals). That way, my sales staff can't get seduced by a mega-account either.

October 23: Cannot sleep again. The good news is, I shook hands today on our new office. It's so beautiful, I can't believe it's ours. It's about two miles from our new house; I could walk to work. It was time to leave the other office. Our landlord kept promising he would clean the halls better, vacuum more frequently. But it never happened. We're renting 1,500 square feet that we can design ourselves in a converted elementary school, and there's pretty glass block in the entryway. The rent is $1,000 per month, but our landlord, Stan F., has agreed to let us pay $800 the first year, $1,000 next year, and $1,200 the third year. I have to sign a lease agreeing to pay $36,000 over three years. But Dwight F. was right: It was easy negotiating with Stan, because his office is on the third floor of our new building. We mortgaged slightly more than that same amount for our house, but to pay over 30 years!

If we continue working on the T—— account (a telemarketing job), that alone can pay all our monthly bills and payroll. The job came from the son of someone I used to work with at W——. When my former colleague and I had lunch one day, he told me what his son did, and I asked if I could call him. But with this additional business and new office come more expenses. Fran needs a more efficient set-up for the callers. We need more mailing equipment for Karen, and Pat needs a nicer desk. We need a clean, bright conference room with a new table and chairs where we can think creatively. Pat is the best at sniffing out auctions and deals, so she's agreed to help me.

I'm also feeling all twisted inside about problems at work. Liza is still not bringing in business. She promised to bring in $30,000 per month to justify her salary, and after four months she has brought in no new business. I'll have to work with her more.

Fran is in a foul mood. She seems angry all the time, but she won't tell me why. I have to deal with her work performance and leave her attitude out of it.

Talked for almost two hours to Mary S. (a very close friend) on the phone. Our longest-running subject was how to live the perfect, stress-free life. I've been holding these words dear: "The perfect life is to live as a poor man does, but have all the money in the world" (Pablo Picasso). Mary and I agreed that money can equal confidence. When you feel there is enough coming in to feel safe, you relax and can be more creative, more thoughtful.

The few times when I do feel safe (after a bunch of checks come in and Pat B. makes the deposit) I feel wonderful, alive, full of energy, uncluttered. That is about 5 percent of the time. The rest of the time I live in constant fear that we are going to disintegrate

---

LESSONS LEARNED

#29: Reducing the Day-to-Day Anxiety

At this point in business, I had still not figured out how to get new business in a controllable fashion. I hadn't learned to concentrate on a few markets and let the synergy of that standard business practice bring in business without trying so hard. By trying to be all things to all markets, I put a strain on operations to "figure out" a new industry every time we brought in a new project.

I also did not have confidence in my own sales ability at this point in the business, which made it hard for me to find a good second salesperson. I didn't know the qualities to look for.

into thin air, that I won't be able to meet payroll or pay our vendors, who are so patient with us.

November 10: Tension in the back of my eyes again. Usually this is related to money. I can feel the calculator in my brain adding up jobs. I know we are pricing these jobs better now (twice as much in receivables as we have in payables), but I'm still not bringing home a paycheck.

November 15: Cool fall Sunday morning. Chill creeps into the house, but it feels good. Took the dogs for an early morning walk. I rarely have time to do this. Last night we saw Darlene, and she talked happily about her new job at A——. She doesn't have to worry about pay because she is on straight salary, not commission. How can A—— be such a flourishing start-up? At first I was mystified. They've only been in business for one year, yet they have more than 20 employees and very beautiful offices.

Darlene doesn't question that. I feel her comparing A—— with us. "After our first year in business, why weren't we as successful at DRM?" I can feel her asking. I do not tell her what I have finally figured out: A—— was started by huge chunks of cash from a parent company. And coincidentally, the parent company is one of their biggest customers. Dar never really understood how that stuff worked, and I didn't want to get into it. It doesn't really matter. I'm glad she's happy and secure. I also didn't tell her that our business is still as stormy and confused as ever.

November 16: I'm still struggling, and it has to do with Liza. I must turn her into a salesperson capable of bringing in $1 million in sales per year and capable of earning $100,000 a year. I want her to feel that we are a company to be proud of. I feel our services are not up to her standards, our name not quite well known enough to give her that extra mantle of credibility. She is so used to working for a "name" company. She is so used to handing over a business card and getting special treatment because of the company she represents.

I also found out, from chatting with her over lunch, that a lot of her accounts were given to her or came in through telephone inquiries. Now she is working for our tiny company, one that most people have never heard of. She's learning how to sell when there

LESSONS LEARNED

#30: The Truths in Business That I Did Not Want to Share With Darlene

Truth #1: The business reflects my personality. If I don't balance my checkbook at home, I don't balance the one at work. If I have a hard time focusing on one household task for long stretches of time, then in business I have a hard time sticking to selling one service. I have a basic lack of understanding of how money and business work together. And my refusal to learn it is hurting the business.

Truth #2: I spend money (such as hiring Liza) without really figuring out where tomorrow's income is coming from. I don't have records to tell me how we are really doing. I make decisions about people and equipment and vendors simply by my gut. And it's not a very experienced gut! I should have allowed six months for Liza to start bringing in business.

Truth #3: My methods of hiring and authorizing hours are random and not really related to people's ability to do jobs. I make decisions about hiring based on helping people find jobs and helping them feel good about themselves, and whether I like and trust them and feel I can work with them.

Truth #4: My understanding of production in direct mail and telemarketing is deeper, broader, and fuller than I will admit. Yet I still pass on that task to someone else so that I can be in sales. I train the operations people inadequately or too quickly. Then I second-guess their decisions, or I look over their output. ("What do you mean this is the direct mail copy for the mailing? Why didn't you incorporate a teaser in the opening line? Why didn't you write it in the first person?")

Truth #5: I find it very hard to deal with people problems. I really let problems simmer until they get good and hot, and then when I finally take care of them, they sometimes explode in my hands.

Truth #6: No matter whether I own this business or work for someone else, these truths will come back to haunt me. I need to change my personality. If I don't I will damage my reputation and my career. Now is the time to begin making the changes.

LESSONS LEARNED

#31: The Real Growth in a Growing Company: Yourself

I have not yet met a hugely successful company that did not have a CEO-founder who had confronted her own strengths and weaknesses. Unless it is a business that stumbled into good fortune (one or two mega-accounts or a niche market with no competition), the CEOs will gladly share what they did wrong and right. These are usually transformed individuals with battle scars. The business has changed them for the better.

---

is no instant name recognition and when the phones are not ringing off the hook.

I talked to Ellice J. about Liza. Since Ellice is such a sharp salesperson, I thought she could give me some insight. Ellice feels Liza might not really have a hunger for money or be driven at all. I think she might be right, but I don't know how to change that. Ellice feels that it is something you are born with.

December 14: Just finished reading *Growing a Business*, by Paul Hawken. He talks about growing a health-food store into a multimillion dollar business, but he doesn't really say step-by-step how he did it. Did he have problems like mine? Our biggest expense is still our "superstar" salesperson, Liza. How can I create a way for her to make us more money? She said she used to bring in $30,000 and $40,000 accounts at D——. Why isn't she doing that for us?

For the last three and half years I have felt that I don't know how to do anything. Every day I discover a little more that I don't know about myself or my skill level. I know my subject; I know my craft. But that just doesn't seem to be enough. I don't know how to run a company and make it successful. I have not mastered that. And a big part of my confidence is tied into knowing what I am doing at work.

January 3: It looks as if I am going to have to get rid of Liza. After spending some time analyzing her in sales meetings, I have to conclude that she doesn't really know how to sell. She doesn't really understand different businesses and how they work. She wants to make a comfortable salary that is similar to what she made at the company she left, but she doesn't really want to work for it. After asking lots of questions, I concluded that she got most of her sales from incoming inquiries at her old company. She didn't really understand cold-call prospecting. I'm going to talk to her and give her two more months. When we move into the new offices at the end of February, we will be paying more rent. I can't pay more rent and pay her. Either she will pay for herself or she will leave.

January 30: Over lunch a friend and I debated the way we approach our daily work. She believes that life is a journey and that you just do your best every day and allow for the fact that people are mortal, so why get excited or set too many goals?

I believe that wanting excellence and order and to be working toward an end result is how we are programmed. It is the only reason to struggle. If we didn't want to strive, there would be no companies employing tens of thousands of people. If we didn't work toward excellence, we would build things that break and not care about it. Who wants to drive a car built by someone with low, let's-give-it-our-best-shot-but-if-we-don't—hey—tomorrow-is-another-day mentality?

February 21: We are getting ready to move into the new office. Pat helped me track down used furniture from a major company in town that closed an office. Bill and his dad installed counters in the telemarketing area that look beautiful and are very flexible. We've been getting more and more business from the telemarketing side of the business. Our TM projects are generating incredible results, while direct mail campaign results have been lackluster.

Mary S. let me hang some of her original art (she's also a well-known local artist). Between her paintings and the plants, it looks like a gallery. We splurged and spent $250 on a new desk for Pat. She deserved it. She is the one handling the calls when we don't pay a bill on time. She's the one who sends out the invoices before she does anything else. (We've worked on this. She knows this is a priority to me.) She now pays all the bills once I okay them (and once we have enough money in the bank!). And she works with the payroll service.

February 28: In thinking about all the people who have influenced me in my life, I realize that I know very few people who are successful and wealthy founders of large companies with lots of employees. Charlie F. wasn't a founder and doesn't create his own products; he sells somebody else's products. Those founders I know are the ones I read about in magazines. I wonder how they really built those companies from scratch.

Moved into our new offices! Felt great!

March 6: Liza is gone. I asked her to leave on Monday. That was my first day in the new office. Bill and I went out for dinner with Darlene and her husband, Bill, and with Dwight F. and his wife, Ruth. I mentally compare Liza with Darlene as the evening unfolds. I also see Darlene's contribution to the company in a better light. Darlene was my strongest ally when I started the business. She rallied behind me when I needed support.

Darlene spent three years doing cold calling on behalf of the company. And it worked; we did get business. She'd get them to a certain point, and I would get them to sign the contract. We were a great team. But I didn't value her because I thought I wanted someone who could do the whole sale, from initial cold call to final contract.

She is happy where she is now, and I have to keep moving forward. With Liza gone, I have my payroll down to a manageable level again. I'm back to being the only one in sales (selling mostly the telemarketing services of our calling staff) without worry about covering the salary of someone who is not making a contribution. It's back to Pat, Colleen, Karen, and Fran, and the telemarketers and me.

With Mike and Liza gone, Colleen is my only back-up to help with direct mail projects.

March 14: Yesterday I met and talked to an exaggerated version of myself. She founded a magazine five years ago. This well-dressed, apparently composed woman told me how she had built a company and then driven it into the ground one month at a time. She was the full-time salesperson, and she had a full-time, salaried office staff. Every month, she would take her publication to the printer, knowing she really didn't have enough in advertising to pay the whole bill and meet payroll. But she did it anyway and hoped that the next month it would be better. And she continued to do that because for some reason she did not want to deal with her problems. She did that for five years.

Today she is calling her lawyer to file for bankruptcy. I've done my share of ignoring the obvious. But I have to keep getting better at dealing with my problems one day at a time. It only took me six months to get rid of Liza. Six months! God.

March 20: First day of spring, and it snowed six inches. Spent the weekend looking at Pat's bookkeeping records. Our greatest source of income and profit is coming from telemarketing. The results we are getting in that area have me excited. It is getting easier for me to talk about that with clients. I am recommending it much more than our direct mail service.

Also opened the one file folder in my office that I've been avoiding for a year: the government file of notices from the Internal Revenue Service. When the IRS envelopes came, Pat would give them to me and I would open them, read again that I owed mounting penalties on the payroll taxes we withheld but did not pay last year and the year before. . . .

It's now up to about $7,000 in taxes and $5,000 in penalties and interest. With Liza off the payroll, I can finally deal with it. We are billing about $20,000 per month, mostly in telemarketing projects that I brought in. I was gambling that her additional sales would help me quickly pay off this tax liability. I was wrong.

March 21: I have to fill out a financial wish list for Lyn D., who wants to be our financial planner. (Barb M. introduced us.) Lyn says we need to decide what our future will look like so that we can set aside money to fund it. Dreaming about the future again. I want to work till I'm 75 but only work three days a week and have the summers off. I want a weekend cottage. I want to have cash reserves for the business equaling at least three times our total liabilities. I want a retirement fund so that I can get income without overburdening the employees who are running the business by then. I want children and the money to send them to college. I want our mortgage to be paid off.

March 26: I have resolved this year to deal squarely with all the "green meanies." That means all the decisions I have postponed because I chose to delay confronting them. Liza was the first. She is gone. Next is sitting down with the IRS and working out a payment plan for the back taxes. That is done. This is an exercise in strength like nothing I've ever done before. While I was on this kick, I also threw out all the papers from our old office, and then I went into the basement of the house and threw away dusty boxes, bottles, and stuff that has been clogging up our lives. . . .

At work Pat ordered a new checking account system, where you make out the check and the carbon completes a bookkeeping entry. We've also switched banks. This bank is closer to our new office. We're finally going to keep track of our expenses without waiting for the accountant to tell us what we did wrong at the end of the year. Pat is going to keep this income statement on a piece of green ledger paper every month. I've paid all my outstanding parking tickets and sat down and recorded all my receipts for the financial statement. I've personally scrubbed down our new office and scrubbed down every room of our house. This feels like a new life. As if we are really getting our act together.

End of Year Four

Years Five and Six: More Stumbling, Changing Direction, and Looking Inward for the Answers

Year Five

Executive Summary

Type of work:	Direct mail services, telemarketing services, telemarketing consulting, design services, mailing lists
Business location:	Moved to new 1,500-square-foot office in converted elementary school, after third year of lease in hotel.
Number of employees:	12 (mostly part-time)
Sources of new business:	Yellow Pages, friends, referrals, repeat customers, word of mouth, networking, newsletter
Investment capital:	Bootstrapping and getting extended credit from vendors
Average monthly sales:	$20,000
Average sale:	$2,500
Annual revenue:	Approx. $260,000
Greatest challenge of the year:	Hiring the ringer
Comments:	First full year doing telemarketing contract work, and it felt great. Also hired a "superstar" salesperson, with disastrous results.

April 6: Calm down, calm down. Totally unable to sleep. We are working on an account that I think may not pay us. It's a telemarketing project, they already owe us $13,000, and I can tell from what they're saying that they don't have the money to pay for it. What have I done?

April 7: Filed this year's tax return. I didn't think I could do it. The records were in shambles. But it is done. I went to a tax service (haven't worked with an accountant in two years because I can't afford one), and for $120 they helped me feel I could cross one more thing off my list.

April 20: Today I'm 32 years old. I know life is short. I wonder what it would be like to live forever? No sense of urgency needed. Take 200, 300 years to figure out this business. It is hard confronting all of my shortcomings so quickly.

April 27: We're not going to get paid by J———. I knew it. They owe us $13,000. Why did we get into this? If Pat and I had had a system for watching how old each outstanding invoice was, we would have stopped doing work for them after they were 45 days overdue. Then we would have only lost $4,000. But it was such a big job, and I was so sure they could handle the bills. I didn't even really talk to them about it until it was too late. Another example of the old way of doing business. I don't have the money to sue them. And even if I won, they couldn't afford to pay me. This means belt-tightening again. We have a little money in savings, and we have other jobs coming in. If this had happened a year ago, it could have put us out of business.

LESSONS LEARNED

#32: How We Should Have Handled the J——— Account

We let this account go too easily. We had a signed contract. We did the work. It was enough money that we should have taken them to court. But I was afraid at the time that if we lost the case (highly unlikely, but always a possibility), I would be out the legal fees as well. We had enough other business coming in that it seemed wiser to move forward.

At this point in business, we should have been following standard collections procedures after 30, 40, 50, 60, etc., days. We would have not lost that much in revenue.

May 1: I realize that the thing about this business that drives me crazy is my inability to consistently decide what business we are in. I have created a company where everything is so up and down that it makes me a little sick. I need some steadiness. Bill gives me that ballast at home. But at work, I'm in charge. Pat provides some ballast, but she's not strong enough to counter my weight. If I charge off in one direction, she may roll her eyes a little but then she follows me shortly afterwards. I want the steadiness of a well-run office. I want reports every day. I want to have staff and production meetings every week at the same time. I want to meet with my clients regularly, and I want a steady flow of income for the business and for myself. But I don't have any of this. And I am the only one who can give it to me.

May 11: Sometimes I get so caught up in the everyday routines of business that I forget how blue the sky can be. I'm having breakfast alone, writing. This issue about steadiness has captured me and repels me. On the one hand it sounds wonderful; on the other it seems crashingly boring. Is there a middle ground?

May 20: It is six hours until the Open House begins at our new offices. I want this to be a crossroad—not in terms of the event itself, but in terms of my ability to manage my business more clearly and more effectively. We have reached a point where we compete in the day-to-day business world here in this business community. Most of our clients are within 25 miles of our office. Some of them (on the telemarketing side, mostly) are the largest companies in the city. We have made mistakes, learned from them, and then lived with them. We have hired expensive people and then gotten rid of them. We have replaced them with harder-working, lesser-paid people. Right now I get $900 per paycheck plus reimbursements for my car payment and expenses.

We are going to start a new chapter in this story.

May 25: First day of vacation in Cape May, back at the bed and breakfast. This time I'm relaxing. There's enough in the bank to cover payroll. Our billings are creeping toward $23,000 and $25,000 per month. It seems that our more profitable, more consistent work is coming from telemarketing. It is easy to measure our performance, and in marketing, that's very important. I've brought along the canceled checks from January through March 31 to look at and analyze. It looks as if our downfall was Liza. If she had not been on the payroll, we would have made a profit. We were spending $3,000 per month on her. We also lost $13,000 on that J—— job. And we moved to a new office and spent some extra money on used furniture.

I chat with Nancy R., the innkeeper. She's very unhappy and wants to make more money. Together we do a cash-flow analysis and marketing plan for attracting corporate customers from Philadelphia and New York. But she doesn't want to hear it. She wants out. Says she will talk to a realtor at the end of the season.

When I hear that people are getting out, I immediately start to count my blessings. I feel I'm on the right track. I don't want to quit. I don't want to fail.

June 26: Work is going so smoothly that it's actually a little boring. Fran knows what to do with the telemarketing jobs. Karen knows what to do with all the direct mail projects. Pat is doing the book-keeping. I've gotten this business off the ground, and it seems to be going okay. I'm not making any money, but I've gotten this train moving forward anyway. This inner boredom never struck me before, and I'm not really sure how to handle it.

July 17: I think it's amazing that we created this business out of thin air. Took an idea and made a business out of it. We are growing, thanks to shifting our services and increasing our average sale. So now comes the next phase. We need to get more business and keep the business we have. I still do a lot of the work, but gradually I'm teaching others to do it for me. And that is easier with telemarketing, because our projects in this area have been very successful. The clients ask fewer questions; they second-guess us less. Our biggest problem is that our direct mail clients don't see us as a telemarketing company, and our tele-marketing clients don't understand that we also offer direct mail services.

July 18: I've started to talk about the business again. In the beginning, I told everyone I had a business, handed out business cards, talked about it at parties. Then gradually, as a I realized how little I really knew, I restrained myself, told no one what I did. If they probed, I told them I was a writer. "Oh that's neat. What do you write about?" "Oh, I write advertising copy." I didn't want to say I owned a direct mail and telemarketing company that was barely getting by, or that I could barely pay my bills and that it only gave me $900 per paycheck. Slowly though, as I've recommitted to making this work, digging in and changing the way I conduct myself in business, I've started telling people again that I'm in business.

July 25: Bills in the envelope waiting to be paid: $4,000. Money sitting in receivables: $11,000. Pat has the two folders sitting on her desk. At night sometimes, after everyone goes home, I sit at Pat's desk and add them up. If the money owed to us is at least two to three times what we owe, I feel safe. If the money owed to us is less than two times what we owe, I utterly panic. It's conditioning from four years of studying those folders. As soon as the money-coming-in folder gets close in size to the money-going-out folder, we go into serious 60- and 90-day periods of hell.

August 15: Just got notified by the state that we need to come up with $10,000 in a bond to continue some of our telemarketing work for nonprofits. Kirk H., our insurance agent, says because of our financial history we will need to provide $10,000 in cash as collateral to get the bond. There is not enough equity in the house. We will have to pull all the money out of savings ($7,500), plus $2,500 from daily income to put up the bond.

August 17: We've been struggling to pay our bills because of taking money out of the checking account for the bond, and because we've lost the T—— business until their budget recycles in four months. It was worth about $8,000 per month.

September 24: Lazy Saturday. Bill has gone golfing with friends, and I have the day to myself. I've left my briefcase at the office. I'm not going to think about work until Monday.

We've turned the corner with the company. The phone seems to be ringing off the hook, and some of my proposals from the summer are starting to turn into contracts. I want so badly to get to a point in the business where the wheels are turning smoothly like

---

LESSONS LEARNED

#33: What Really Changed?

I really feel that narrowing our line of services was the first step toward becoming profitable. Until this point, I was selling whatever people wanted to buy (in the area of marketing and advertising services). With the move toward a few services, and services that I was starting to feel more comfortable about, we started getting more repeat business.

At this point, however, we were still company-dependent on project work. So that meant I rarely relaxed. I was always out looking for the next project.

---

this all the time. I think we're going to hit $40,000 this month in billings, most of it from this telemarketing service.

November 1: I think I've found our next sales rep. She's affordable (she needs a $20,000 annual draw versus Liza's $36,000, and she has telemarketing experience and sales experience). She's a client. Hmmm.

November 2: Crossroads with Bill's mom: Dad took her to the hospital. She's not doing well. Crossroads with the business: Switching services is costing us clients, and it is hard to walk away from that business.

November 14: Have been doing a good job bringing in business, but now having a tough time servicing it. I have P., a client, calling wanting to know what is going on because his project is not going well. Fran is not really skilled at handling clients when there's a problem (the real test of whether you have a good employee). I'm not sure Colleen is mature enough to handle working with clients alone, either. She is fine when she does what I tell her, but she's still very young. We are having turnover in telemarketing. I think Fran could be a better manager than she is. Her callers are not working the hours they promise, so we're losing billable hours.

November 21: Hired our next sales rep. Patti J. is a former client and used to be the manager of a telemarketing department. So she understands the industry. She also has had lots of sales experience with a radio station. She started last week. She already knows our work from being a client, so she can start selling right away.

December 1: Colleen resigned. She's going to work for her father in his new business. He left the business that he founded with his brother to start the new company. In his old company his average sale was $10,000. In the new company his average sale will be $200,000. He told me he no longer thinks that the number of employees is a measure of success. Employees are a headache. He said he's going to keep his next company small and hire subcontractors. Sounds very tempting.

December 16: Bill's mom is dying, and there is nothing we can do for her. Nothing else seems remotely important. I adore this woman and cannot think about work, yet I know everyone is counting on me.

December 21: I've spent the last two days with Bill's family, huddled outside his mother's hospital room or in the cafeteria. Pat is here also. We are on a skeleton staff until after the first of the year because this is a slow time for us, so I don't feel I need to be at work. Pat and I sit in the cafeteria at the hospital after spending 24 hours together. It's the first time in the last two days that she mentions work.

In the years we've worked together, Pat has had difficulty telling me how to conduct my business. I am the one who probes and asks questions when I sense something is wrong. Sometimes I wait too long before asking; this is one of those times. She has been frustrated with Fran for months and hinting that something was wrong. Pat admits as carefully as she can that she thinks Fran is running her own telemarketing company while working for us. And worse yet, she is getting our employees to cut their hours with us to work for her and her clients.

I always brag that I have a very long wick and rarely get angry. But here in the hospital cafeteria I can feel a rock in my throat. I can barely speak, and I end the conversation quickly. I don't need to hear anymore. It is 1:30 in the afternoon. I do not explain to anyone; I go to my car, drive to work, and storm into the office. Fran has been keeping an eye on things while we've been at the hospital; she is on the phone when I walk into her office. No one else is around, so I do not need to shut the door.

"I am no longer in need of your services. Give me your keys, get your purse, and I will walk you out." I can barely get the words out of my throat, I am so furious. She says carefully that she would like an explanation. "I no longer need your services," I repeat. The entire incident takes less than 10 minutes. I call the locksmith and ask that the locks be changed immediately. Patti is there, and we talk briefly. I ask her to put an ad in the paper every Sunday for the next three Sundays. We will need to hire eight people. I wait for less than an hour and the locksmith arrives. While I wait, I call and leave messages or speak personally to the eight telemarketers who Fran hired. Each one gets the same explanation: "I am no longer in need of your services. You will get your last paycheck mailed to you next Friday."

Then I call the last remaining telemarketer, Janet. We hired her two weeks ago after advertising in the paper. Pat feels she wasn't involved with Fran's company. I ask Janet about it, and she admits knowing what was going on, but she was new, and so the only person she told was Pat. I ask if she can serve as temporary manager when she returns in January. She agrees. Then the locksmith hands me the new keys, I give Patti a key and instructions to lock the office behind her, and I drive back to the hospital. I am reeling. I have client projects restarting in January. I have one telemarketer.

I tell Pat and Bill what I've done when I get back to the hospital at 4:30 P.M., but we do not discuss it. That's not Pat's style or mine. Mom dies at 6:55 P.M. the same day. Empty holes everywhere I turn. She wanted her kids to be happy. Can't bear the thought of life without her.

January 2: Been terribly depressed. I've been fighting it, but it keeps coming back in waves. Have customers and employees counting on me.

Must hire people to replace the telemarketers I fired. Fortunately, we normally lay off our callers during the holidays because it's not a good time to call businesses. But this is my chance to rethink the business again. Offering telemarketing was a good decision. But I'm still tormented by this issue about taking responsibility for so many people and so much payroll. I stayed out of Fran's way, and she took advantage of me. Pat doesn't want to manage these people while I'm out of the office selling. Do I stay committed to moving in this direction?

January 11: Took the morning off to try to shake off these continuing feelings of depression and sort out my decision about the telemarketing department. I've been talking a lot to Patti over the last few months. She believes strongly in affirmations and self-improvement. If I choose to think positively about the business, I can say, "I made over $250,000 last year. I just chose to spend $249,000 of it."

January 12: I am hiring new callers. We have clients who count on us. I would be starting all over again, and I can't bear the thought of going backwards. Janet is helping me screen and hire the new staff. She has a ton of telemarketing experience and may be the next manager. In the meantime, Patti is helping hire too, in addition to selling. One of the new callers, Judy K., has secretarial experience. She also agrees to back up the reception desk when needed.

January 18: Patti suggests that we redo our brochure. She thinks we should broaden our services. She knows radio and thinks we could sell radio commercials and production. Also wants to get into other media advertising, public relations. That was the area of advertising that I was trained in, and it sounds tempting because we can bill for more money. I'll let her do it and see what happens.

January 17: On being an owner: Unless you started something completely on your own, invented it, then sold it, and sold it some more, then made mistakes and learned from them, you can't understand what we've gone through. Patti doesn't understand. I know how much we want in sales, but I haven't figured out how to get there. She says maybe I don't think I deserve to be successful.

January 22: Barb M. and I meet to exchange Christmas gifts—a month late, since the holidays were so strange. She gives me a book she found at the bookstore: *Living a Beautiful Life,* by Alexandra Stoddard. I sit down to read it as soon as I come home. It is about a way of living that is remote to me. The author talks about creating beautiful daily rituals to enrich each day, like having fresh flowers on your desk at work. She talks about living each day deeply and well and with solid meaning, rather than rushing around fragmented.

So if I were going to create this beautiful work life for myself, what would it contain? No bills, no bills, no bills, no bills, savings, savings, savings, savings, income, income, income, income.

She says to treat yourself and those around you with grace and dignity. I haven't been doing that. I've been frenzied, fractured, running, thinking, and plotting the future. I want to have this life she talks about in the book. I thought I was "earning points" by doing without, waiting until everything was perfect before I relaxed and enjoyed what I had. That kind of stinginess says that we must suffer until we have earned a certain amount of money, and then we can relax and enjoy it. But Ms. Stoddard encourages her readers not to wait for the perfect moment to celebrate. I do have a tendency to race through life. The days get gobbled up unless I slow them down myself. Time to live a civilized, orderly life before it runs away from me. I wrote Alexandra a letter last night telling her how much I loved her book.

February 5: Reading a book by David Ogilvy on advertising and owning an agency. He says in an employee manual, "If you always hire people who are smaller than you, we shall become a company of dwarfs. If you always hire people who are bigger than you, we shall become a company of giants." That sounds great. But part of my problem is I can only afford dwarfs.

February 6: For me to make more money, I have to make sure Patti meets her $20,000-per-month quota.

February 11: I can't get this book, *Living a Beautiful Life,* out of my head. I think I've been feeling that the company had me sucked into a hole. I haven't thought about anything else in years. Even Bill's mother's illness didn't keep me from going to work.

In her book, Alexandra talks about slowing down long enough to observe all the details of your life, and make them pleasing to you, orderly, well-maintained. This applies to how you deal with people as well as things. I rush through life. We have good friends, but I never see them. I love my family, but I'm too busy to talk to them. I could do a better job relating to my employees, but I'm too busy rushing past them to take care of a customer. I'm too busy to enjoy a project or a customer because I feel I have to rush to the next one to get everything done in a day.

So in a way, I have pushed myself into the ocean and am holding my own head under water. Time to stop.

February 12: I don't think it is an accident that I met and hired Patti and was given Alexandra Stoddard's book. I have been acting, doing, almost without thinking for five years. I am afraid to look too closely at myself for fear of what I will find. I feel I am beginning a new journey.

February 24: I think I know what I want for a change. I want my life to be serene and productive and fun. I want the business to be profitable and worth my time. I don't know how to get there. I've been searching for help in books. It's hard explaining to family and friends that you are trying to live a beautiful life at home and at work.

Been reading another book Barb M. gave me: *How to Get Control of Your Time and Your Life,* by Alan Lakein. Through a series of exercises, you write down all the really important things you want to accomplish. Then he guides you to develop a bridge between where you are and where you want to be. He calls them action steps. So if I want to build a successful company and a more balanced life, I'm going to have to work with Patti to increase her sales. I must do a survey of other telemarketing companies and look at our pricing. And I'm going to have to start going home without a briefcase more often.

February 28: Did a quick survey of other agencies in the city. Also talked to Bill K., who owned the typesetting company. He lost his biggest client and is struggling. They were bought out by a larger firm, and a downtown advertising agency pitched for and won the account. Bill is now typesetting anything he can get his hands on, including menus for restaurants. But he does share his advertising design prices with me. We are undercharging by as much as 50 percent! The same is true when I survey telemarketing companies in other cities. No wonder we are not making any money. New pricing. I take our price list and make the changes myself. I will meet with everyone tomorrow.

March 1: Patti loaned me a little book about money and the emotional issues wrapped around it, called *Money Is My Friend*, by Phil Laut. It is very short and easy to read, and it digs right into the heart of my problem. I don't think I deserve to be successful! And I have a lot of negative feelings about money. In one of the exercises from the book, I made a list of all my feelings about money:

1. I never have enough of it.
2. I spend more than I make.
3. I feel guilty charging prices equal to other companies' because I'm not sure we are worth it.
4. I feel guilty spending money on myself.
5. I think that no true wealth comes without struggle (easy come, easy go).
6. I think that to really deserve wealth, I must do everything perfectly.
7. I think that nothing good comes easy.
8. I think that if I make too much money, people won't like me anymore.
9. I think that if I make too much money, I will do stupid things with it.
10. I think that if I make too much money, I will have to take care of other people who have less, and I don't want that responsibility.
11. I think that if I become truly successful, I stand an even bigger chance of being a high-profile failure.

After doing this exercise, I have to write an affirmation next to each one. So I write:

1. I always have enough money for anything I need.
2. I always have a little more than I can possibly spend.
3. We are worth every penny that we charge.
4. I spend money on myself easily and without guilt.

5. Making money comes easily and without effort.
6. I make money easily by trying my best and truly caring about my customers.
7. Good things come into my life easily and without effort.
8. Money has nothing to do with friendship. Good friends will support all my efforts, and I will support theirs.
9. Everything I spend money on comes back to me tenfold. I learn from every experience.
10. I make enough money to give it away willingly to anyone who needs it, without care, because every time I give money away it comes back to me tenfold.
11. I will live in this life learning from everything I do, and that learning will not interfere with my ability to be successful and prosperous in this world.

I rewrite this on a small piece of paper and put in my wallet.

LESSONS LEARNED

#34: On Your Feelings About Prosperity and How They May Affect Your Business

Patti was right. I didn't think I deserved to be successful. I'm still not completely sure why. But for me, it was most important to recognize what I was doing to myself, my family, my employees, and my customers through this attitude. My personal way of working through this was to regularly list my negative feelings about money as an "attitude check." It took almost two years for the list of negative feelings to disappear. The negative attitude I found hardest to shake was: "Nothing good in life comes easily." I think I was making this business more of a personal challenge than it needed to be.

In my travels, I've met a lot of people running what they consider to be unsuccessful businesses, and this subject seems to draw the most emotional response in conversation. I'm always surprised to find that I am not alone.

March 6: I have to find a way to get Patti to go on more appointments. She is pretty good when she goes on sales calls. Her background in radio advertising prepared her well. She is organized, systematic, and comfortable making cold calls and getting contracts. But her personal life is a mess. She spends half her life on the phone arguing with family members. She is planning a wedding. She is trying to buy a house. She doesn't go on enough appointments.

I also have to lay off Karen. We are doing so much more telemarketing that I don't need her direct mail skills. I have to get Pat to become more comfortable with the computer so that she can get our accounting onto it. I have to be more aggressive and not wait for business to come to me. I have to go out and find it.

March 8: I talk to Patti, cut Karen's hours in half (don't have the nerve to lay her off completely), and talk to Pat. No one is happy.

March 11: Patti came to the house, and we talked about the future of the company. What is my vision, she asked? I struggled with the answer. I think we want to keep on offering our direct mail and

---

LESSONS LEARNED

#35: Meandering From My Own Vision

Yes, I did let my own employees talk me out of sitting alone long enough to figure out where I wanted to go. I did it with Darlene, I did it with Liza, and I did it again with Patti—all three salespeople drew on their own backgrounds and expertise to decide what business they would and could bring to my company.

I was so preoccupied with the idea of being in business, I neglected to be completely sure of what business I was in. In some ways, I had been running two businesses concurrently for the last five years: my business, and the business my employees saw. My personal vision wasn't focused enough. I saw possibility in every idea. That meandering of vision dragged me through more trouble than I needed to endure.

telemarketing services. She wants to do public relations and advertising because she is comfortable with those methods. I think the results from those methods are harder to measure, which is why I've always promoted DM and TM. But I agree to let her sell them as long as she manages those contracts. She agrees.

March 25: Nothing else matters to me as much right now as making this business work out.

End of Year Five

Year Six

Executive Summary

Type of work:	Telemarketing services, direct mail services, mailing lists
Number of employees:	12 (mostly part-time); let eight people go at the end of the year
Business location:	Converted elementary school, 1,500 square feet
Source of new business:	Prospecting through a second sales-person, referrals, word of mouth, newsletter
Capital sources:	No new investment capital
Average monthly sales:	$20,000
Average sale:	$2,500
Annual revenue:	Appr. $270,000
Greatest challenge of the year:	This was the height of my confusion. I began a sincere personal journey to try to find the true business I wanted to be in and to find myself in the process.
Comments:	I had been in business more than five years. I was supposed to make money, have fun, get ahold of the business. But I kept changing our services and putting our customers into a state of confusion. What business was Anita in, anyway?

April 3: I'm searching for another way to live that is not so crazy. The author of the book *Living a Beautiful Life* is coming out with another book. I have kept her book near me for the last three months. She described a world I am not familiar with, where there is time to sit and drink iced tea with fresh mint and read favorite books a second time. She also owns a business, has two children and a good marriage, writes books, and seems to love and enjoy life. She's even found time to send me three letters in response to mine. So if I know one person can do it, then I know it is possible. Other than her, though, I can't think of a soul I know who is living this life.

April 5: Because of work I was doing for C. (a client), I was referred to another client. We are now doing work for them, and I've been asked if I would speak to her professional organization. I haven't spoken in public in years, but I want to help the business any way I can. So here I am at the library to work on my speech and read books about public speaking. Time to take a public-speaking class.

April 25: The rent is paid. Payroll was three days ago, and we made it easily. These are times when I feel guilt-free, tension-free, clear-headed. I've been successfully selling the telemarketing services. Patti is still not generating the sales she promised, but I say very little about it. Okay, keep moving forward.

May 20: Gave my speech. It went well, and I feel we can help some of the people who came to the meeting. I am in the right field. I just have to enjoy it more.

May 21: Message on a tea bag: "Businesses don't fail. The owner quits."

May 31: Weekend in Cape May. Nancy has the inn for sale and is carrying around brochures for a round-the-world cruise. Her asking price is $750,000. She wants to retire at age 46 and enjoy the rewards of the 24-hour-a-day, seven-day-a-week, nine-months-a-year life she's led for the last eight years. We do not talk about marketing. She's leaving that up to the next owner.

June 11: Got a call from H———. They attended the speech and liked what I said and want a proposal.

June 12: On Thursday night, I gently told Karen I was laying her off. She took it personally, and I know she was devastated after giving me loyal service for the last three years. She was a friend of one of Darlene's neighbors and worked for me when we got a direct mail job. Then she was around all the time because we were doing a lot of direct mail, and so I made her a full-time employee. But since we've been doing more and more telemarketing and less direct mail, she's been stretching her work to fill her days.

Pat asked for a meeting to show me the books and point out what she has been telling me through the weekly management reports. Our expenses for Patti's guaranteed salary come unrelentingly every month without the sales to offset them. And the services she does sell have slimmer profit margins. So the $12,000 she brings in per month yields us less money to pay bills because it is not telemarketing or direct mail. It is time to also look at Patti, she says. Pat tells me she has been fielding an enormous number of personal calls for Patti since the beginning of the year.

June 27: Patti got us a presentation with a local hospital through a referral from her friend at M——. It's for more media advertising, and Patti says she'll handle all of it. I'm comfortable with that decision. Besides, she knows that side of advertising much better than I do. She put the entire proposal together and it was perfect when I checked it. I'm taking a risk letting her pull the company in a new direction. But I'm working on my own accounts (mostly telemarketing), and it is a relief to work with someone who is self-sufficient (is it possible to get the perfect salesperson?), even if she isn't giving me 100 percent of her attention. . . .

June 28: Summer is here. The roses are blooming and we've had nights hot enough that Bill and I have started sitting on the front porch together at night talking. I found a small table lamp and ran it to the porch with an extension cord. It reminds me of the Cape May bed and breakfast porch. I've been slowly working on every room of the house and every room in our office, doing the same thing: making the room feel homey, warm, comfortable.

July 13: Weird at work. Even with Patti not bringing in the business, all our bills are paid. We took care of every single one. We have money to meet payroll. We have money in the cash reserve fund. We are up to 70 percent telemarketing and 30 percent for combined direct mail, lists, consulting, media advertising, general advertising, and public relations. The telemarketing accounts are all mine, and about half the other business is also. Patti is still developing her own clients. Slow going for her.

July 19: Leaving for Nova Scotia in a few days to see Holley and Bill. Holley worked for me and Darlene at W—— for four months as a summer intern, and we've kept in touch ever since. This is the trip we wanted to take last year and couldn't because of money problems with the business.

July 30: Crewed for Holley and Bill in a sailboat race; we came in first in our class. I've never won anything so easily before. It feels good to win! And it was not an accident. Holley's husband, Bill, is a fantastic sailor, and he knew exactly what he was doing during the whole race. Is that what it feels like in business when you know what you are doing?

August 3: Came back having decided we need to spend weekend time doing more than running errands and me doing paperwork. Is a weekend cottage too much to hope for?

August 15: Have come to a crossroads with Patti. Our agreement was that I would pay her a draw of $2,000 per month against commissions. In exchange she would bring in $20,000 per month in new business. She isn't doing it. So far she has been averaging about $12,000 per month since she started nine months ago. She's angry with me. She has been working on a major account, more than $200,000, which is mostly media advertising and direct mail. Says it will come in any day now. I agree to wait but ask her to start working on developing smaller accounts with less turnaround time because we need the billings.

August 16: Last night was one of the most interesting nights of my life. Barb M. (my good friend) called me and asked if I wanted to be on a miniboard of directors for our friend Lyn D.(a financial planner). She called it a "self-board." Our first meeting was at my house. We were on the front porch until almost 3 A.M., with the little table lamp shining over us while we sat in the wicker rockers

talking. When it got chilly, I pulled out the blankets and we huddled under them while we continued to talk. We've decided that it
isn't enough to set your own goals. You have to share them with
people you trust. So this self-board is a way to share our dreams
out loud. This is the first time I have ever done that: shared
dreams out loud. Barb and Lyn have their dreams too. So our
assignments were distributed at the end of the night. We will help
each other achieve our goals.

August 21: We got H—— as a new account! The ones who heard
me speak at the professional meeting. And they are wonderful people besides!

LESSONS LEARNED

#36: An Important Exercise to
De-Stress Your Life

During this journey of self-exploration, I came across a book that recommended I simply list all the things in my life that were causing me
stress. Then underneath each one, I should list the things I needed to
change to cross it off the list.

For example, I felt chronic stress from never having enough
money to pay bills. So my list included:

Checking pricing offered by our competitors. (That helped me
    discover we were underpricing the services we offered.)
Asking for larger up-front deposits.
Using Pat to track all income and expenses per job so that I
    could see every week where the money was going.
Asking Pat to help control expenses by writing all the checks
    and taking that out of my hands.
Concentrating on our telemarketing service, which was well-
    received in the marketplace and got great results for our cus-
    tomers. (As a result, repeat business started flowing in.)

Identifying the stressors and dealing with them instead of suffering
chronic anxiety was a big change for me.

August 30: Have spent the last eight months trying to figure out why I make life's rewards so difficult to achieve. Before this year, I felt as though I were chasing my tail. We had lots of bills. I was always vaguely unhappy. Thanks to these self-board meetings with Barb and Lyn, I'm learning to admit what I don't know out loud, instead of just writing it here in the diary.

September 13: Talked to Barb M. on the phone for two hours. We are both so excited about this self-board!

September 19: More telemarketing projects coming in from our Yellow Pages advertising, and my networking and speaking. I had a long talk with Janet (our telemarketing manager). We could lose her. She says she can make more money at another telemarketing company, and we don't pay benefits. I have to do things differently. I have always wanted everything in my company to be different from the way it is in the rest of the world. Janet told me what is missing in the industry: full-time jobs where a person can earn $20,000 per year and benefits and vacations, etc. To keep three good people would cost me $60,000 plus benefits and taxes. I would need to charge more. But for that, what could I offer clients in return? Better quality calling. And with little turnover, we would be unstoppable. I'd have to absorb the risk and bring in enough business on a regular basis to guarantee full-time work to my staff. I think I can sell this.

And I think I talked Janet into staying.

October 13: Yesterday was an incredible day. We received four contracts totaling $40,000 in one day. They were all telemarketing projects. I did read that once we accepted wealth and prosperity, it would come pouring in. Okay, okay, it's a little hokey, but it may be working.

November 2: Christmas coming. It will be the first one without Bill's mom. Sad and joyful at the same time. She loved Christmas.

November 13: Coming to the end of our third year in this office. There's a building for sale less than a mile away. It is a quaint building, but old. They want $85,000 for it. But Bill's dad says it will need a double furnace, and a contractor estimates it will cost

$200,000 to fix it up the way we want to. I can imagine us there, but I will not put us in a bad financial situation to get it.

November 18: Self-board meeting at Lyn's house. An incredible night. We were talking about the power of knowing what you want and asking for it out loud. We decided to ask for something specific that we could all work on: a piece of the Berlin Wall. We agreed on setting a time limit: getting it in 30 days. Then Lyn immediately called her cousin in Frankfurt, Germany. His wife answered. He had to leave on an assignment and won't be home for a few weeks. That was okay, we had 30 days.

I got home at 2 A.M., and Bill woke up when I crawled into bed. I told him we were trying to get a piece of the Berlin Wall in 30 days. He kind of laughed and went back to sleep. At 9:30 A.M. I got a call from Bill at work. At 8:30 he had told his coworkers what we were doing, and someone said they had heard a radio interview with a man who was importing pieces of the wall to sell in the United States. Bill gave me the name of the radio station. By 10 A.M. I had placed an order for three pieces of the Berlin Wall for $8.95 apiece!

Are we able to get what we want simply if we know what we want?

November 30: Got my pieces of the Berlin Wall. They come in little blue velvet sacks and don't look authentic.

December 12: Lyn opened her mail yesterday and there was a package from her cousin in Frankfurt. He had gotten the message but never called back. Instead, he just wrapped up a piece of the Berlin Wall and sent it to Lyn. She is breaking it into three pieces. It is 29 days from our self-board meeting.

December 16: For two days, Barb M., Lyn D., and I rented a large room at the V. Hotel to talk about our goals for the coming year. We brought fruit and juice and lots of paper and only left the room to eat dinner and work out at the fitness center. I brought my diary. Our assignment was to write down what we wanted to accomplish in our lifetime and how that related to our goals for the coming year.

December 18: Why is it so hard to talk about our goals out loud? When I was little, my mother told me it was bragging to tell people what you were trying to accomplish—even worse, that your goal could get jinxed if you talked about it out loud (blow out the candles, but don't tell anyone your wish or it won't come true!). These meetings with these two women are the only places where I can talk about what I want and not be judged.

At the end of the weekend, we decide that one of our goals this year is to try working on a project together. Lyn has a neat business idea that she started 10 years ago for a brief time. We want to look at it again as a three-way partnership. It would require work over and above our full-time jobs. We are excited about combining our energy and talent to produce something together.

December 27: It's the end of the year already. I am clearer about what I want. In a way, it is scary how powerful our minds really are. Like homing devices on a nuclear warhead: Just tune in to the destination and then get out of the way.

January 12: From all the goal setting, I have drafted a mission statement . . . kind of a Life's Purpose. Mine is to help people and their businesses to grow financially.

January 15: Had our second production meeting of the year with staff. I used to have these meetings sporadically. But everyone complained that they could never reach me to get questions answered. So we're meeting every week for about an hour. They love these regular meetings. I still find it difficult to concede to a scheduled meeting, but I am trying. Patti and Pat and Janet tell me what happened in their areas the week before and what will be happening in the coming week. I've designed a weekly management report to reduce the amount of talking, and that tells me what we billed for the past week, how much we owe others in total, and how much all our outstanding receivables are. Before the meeting, Janet fills in data on the report on how many billable hours we had in telemarketing. Patti fills in how many contracts came in the week before and who we have outstanding proposals with. It's all on one sheet of paper so that I can look at how we are doing compared to the week before. I read a book about a guy who managed a multinational company with 18 subdivisions in a similar fashion. Why not?

January 28: Just found out that Patti's contact at M—— was fired suddenly. We asked for a meeting to see how it affects the project. This account is worth $200,000, and we are only $50,000 into it.

January 30: Another self-board meeting with Lyn and Barb. We talked about all the material things we'd like to have when we are wealthy. But I am having difficulty with this. What is next? What do you do after you have the house and the car and the stuff? We didn't come up with any good answers in the group. I'm going to have to come up with some goals of my own, because money for money's sake just isn't enough. Actually, that was the same difficulty I had when I talked with Ellice J., Phil B., and Charlie F. On the one hand, I sensed that their success was tied to a drive and sense of urgency that had nothing to do with money. But in the end, they kept score with the money, and that seemed like placing importance on the wrong values. I need to keep on focusing on what I really want—which is a serene life, a small mortgage, a

---

LESSONS LEARNED

#36: The Power of the Self-Board

When Barb and Lyn asked me to be a part of these regular group meetings, I had no idea what I was getting into. They called it a board of directors for yourself, or a *self-board*, to use Barb's word. Indeed, we met regularly to admit our hopes and dreams and ask for guidance and support. All three of us owned our own businesses, and all three of us felt we were not as far along as we thought we should be. A personal board of directors seemed like a neat way to get there.

For the first time, I was able to admit my hopes and dreams outside the safety of my marriage. I admitted that I wanted to be more successful in business than I was. Lyn and Barb shared their dreams as well. It was the beginning of a new way of operating. I didn't have to have all the answers. It was a feeling of relief.

weekend cottage, children, a happy marriage, clients who love us and stay with us for years, and employees who do the same.

February 11: Signed all the papers on a $12,000 loan with the bank to consolidate all my credit card debt from the business. It was Barb M.'s idea from the self-board meetings. We'll repay it over three years. I feel much better about this than paying the outrageous interest I was paying by maintaining $12,000 of debt on credit cards. Even since we started working with this new bank, they have been wonderful to deal with. Carol M., the branch manager, got me the loan with very little hassle.

February 18: Have decided to postpone buying a building. Our toilets backed up, and I watched our landlord and his son stare at the creeping brown stain under the carpet. They got nothing done for two days while they waited for the plumber to tell them how much it would cost to fix the problem. Did someone plan this? I don't have that kind of time . . . or money. Time to renew our lease.

Our newest, biggest account, M——, is canceled. Patti is philosophical. I am not so casual. We needed those billings, and Patti doesn't really have much other business in her pipeline.

February 21: We renewed the lease for another three years. I ask our landlord if we can keep the same rate and would he paint the walls and build a storage closet for us? He agrees to everything and offers to split the cost of the closet. For another three years we can concentrate on building the company and not worry about toilets backing up or leaky roofs. Besides, the more I think about it, the cost of moving and changing our address and phone number mean we will lose some momentum.

March 3: I've been taking one Monday a month as a quiet, library day. I take all my paperwork, personal paperwork, correspondence, and my journal and head for the main library. It is huge and old and a little dark. But the section where I settle down (art and art history) has tall windows and 20-foot ceilings and is rarely busy. I carry a tote bag so large I usually have to carry it with two hands. This is where I can work on proposals for new projects and plan ahead for the company.

March 4: Had a terrible self-board meeting last night. Very disappointing. We spent most of it talking about this new business idea we had developed at our overnight session in the hotel in December. Last night Barb asked to drop from the self-board group. Said she hated start-ups and was finding the drive inconvenient. The fragile trust we had formed to share our dreams might be over.

March 19: The power of ritual. The woman who wrote *Living a Beautiful Life* says that daily rituals are comforting, bring order and joy, and sustain you. I can only think of one person who seemed to ritualize his work: Charlie F., the guy who ran the super-successful insurance agency. He arrived at the office the same time every day, had open-door periods every day, and ate at the same club with different people almost every day for breakfast and lunch. I haven't talked to him in over a year . . . since our consulting project was finished. But I can see now how his rituals kept him clearheaded to focus better on problems.

I am establishing my own rituals. My days are spent being available to staff, seeing clients, and talking to clients by phone. At night I do my paperwork, read the mail, keep up with my other reading, write proposals, correspond with clients.

I'll work on fresh mint in the iced tea next year.

March 28: I have been maintaining a positive attitude and feeling good about the business. But the truth is, our payables are mounting steadily. January and February are usually slow times for our project-driven business. Patti brought in one major account in the last six months (supposed to be worth more than $200,000), and now that our client was let go, his boss has canceled their contract. The other account she has is one I gave her. I have to reduce our expenses, and her draw is the place I want to do it. Here we go again. . . .

Pat and I reviewed our payables. Pat offered to cut back on her hours until the billings went back up. I accepted the offer. I can't believe how lucky I am to have her. Janet agreed to cut her supervisory time to 10 hours per week and spend 30 hours per week on the phone as a caller.

My meeting with Patti didn't go as well. I told her we were really in the midst of a crisis, that I would stop paying her a guaranteed salary by the end of April. She said that the reason she hasn't been selling is that she was too busy servicing the M——— account. I told her maybe it is not fair to have her selling and servicing, but I can't afford to do it any other way. I give her 30 more days on probation to bring in $23,000 as she promised.

My conclusion is, the company can survive almost anything. I just have to stay on top of everything and make decisions quickly. The longer I linger in decision making, the more it hurts the company.

[Note: Talked to Lyn about compensation for salespeople. She's been in sales for years and told me I had structured Patti's pay incorrectly. I should have put a limit on her draw. In other words, I offered to pay her a $2,000-per-month draw against commission. But I didn't put a limit on how long she could draw without adequate commissions to cover the draw. Had I put a limit of, say, $5,000 on her draw, she would have known she could only take $5,000 in salary from the company without bringing in any sales. The way I set it up, she was making $2,000 regardless of what she brought in for the month. And even though I gave her a report every month that said she was "overdrawn" by a certain number of dollars, she got a check anyway. I don't think she even read the report. With Lyn's way, both you and your salesperson are watching the kitty. There is only $5,000 in it. When that is used up, the salesperson stops collecting a check. The way to help a new salesperson is to give her a few house accounts so that she can at least get some credit for sales from the start.]

End of Year Six

Years Seven, Eight, and Nine: Looking Outward and Getting More Answers; Building a Foundation

Year Seven

Executive Summary

Type of work:	Telemarketing, direct mail, media, advertising, design, public relations (expanded services around Patti's background in radio and television advertising and public relations)
Number of employees:	12 (mostly part-time telemarketers rehired after the Fran disaster)
Business location:	Converted elementary school, 1,500 square feet
Sources of new business:	Referrals, word of mouth, newsletter, and Patti doing prospecting and networking
Capital sources:	No new investment capital; debt consolidation of $12,000 in credit card debt
Average monthly sales:	$30,000
Average sale:	$3,500
Annual revenue:	Approx. $370,000
Greatest challenge of the year:	Personal journey to change my feelings about money and life
Comments:	Spent most of the year on another detour (media advertising and public relations) after concentrating on telemarketing and direct mail for a year.

117

April 4: Spent the day at the library. I love this part of my work. A client, R——, has come to me with a tricky marketing challenge. They are an environmental testing company and they want a creative marketing solution involving direct mail and telemarketing. I think I've got one. We're going to test it and then do a roll-out this summer. I'm really excited. I know it's a winner.

April 5: We're working on a huge proposal for a local college worth more than $200,000 that is due in a few days. We were invited to bid after I met a woman at a golf class and she invited me to do some consulting work for her. Then our name appeared on the vendor list for her company, and we've received two invitations from other divisions to bid on major work. We lost the first bid. Now we are bidding on this business. The work will require expertise that I do not have but Patti does (media advertising, etc.). Since she is on probation, I am doing this with trepidation. Not sure of the right thing to do.

April 10: Been working with a new client, Jan R. She is only 24 years old but has more self-confidence and business savvy than I've ever seen in a woman her age. She's a marketing consultant who specializes in real estate marketing. Here it is again: Focus on a single service with a single group of customers. But to me it seems too risky to put all your eggs in one basket. We are helping her with the direct mail for a new shopping center. She found us through a woman I went to college with who knows we specialize in direct mail and telemarketing.

Have I strayed too far from my original mission again? I think so. I don't want this huge account, I realize. And I don't want Patti or anyone telling me what services we will specialize in. We have to narrow our range of services around my expertise. Period. Or we are not going to flourish.

April 23: For a long time I have been angry at all the mouths I have to feed (employees on payroll). But I've come to the realization that I don't have to take care of anyone. The guidelines for success are not measured by the number of employees we have. I can revert to being a consultant and a broker of other services. I chose this route. And the people who work for me take some of the responsibility for our success. But I owe them more leadership than I've been giving them.

April 24: Patti quit today. She is bitter that I changed the rules on her by telling her I was stopping her draw next week when her probation is over. We won't know about this bid for another month, and she still has not been pursuing other proposals. I don't think she believed I would actually cut off her draw. I had to call the college and withdraw from the bidding process because if we had gotten the account, we wouldn't have been able to service it. Our contact said she understood and thanked me.

April 25: Patti came in to get her things. It was a sad day. I'm not used to bad endings. But I did learn some very important things from Patti, about money and my negative attitudes about it. She was forthright and honest and wanted to talk about the problems at hand. She was dogged and determined when she set her mind to something. Unfortunately she was unable to give this stint 100 percent of her attention. In lots of ways I'll miss her.

May 13: Feel sick. Not sure if it is from the stress of bills with little new business in sight to compensate for it. Or am I pregnant? Suppose I am not able to go out and sell every day because of a pregnancy. There are times when I dream of working from home again as a consultant. But if I am pregnant, that plan has a flaw. If something happens to me, I can't serve my clients and can't keep employing Pat. There are no easy answers.

May 14: The last five months our billings have been less than $12,000 per month, and we've had higher expenses on jobs . . . especially Patti's jobs. It isn't fun when we don't have money. But I'm getting better at responding to need. Patti's off the payroll and that helps. Pat is working reduced hours. Janet is putting more billable time in her schedule instead of doing supervisory work. I have to stick to this until all the over-30-day bills get paid and we stabilize. Do not incur any new debt. Do not punish myself by working crazy hours. We just need more projects.

May 15: Victory! I'm getting another car. A jeep with 15,000 miles on it, for only $8,000. Something great, and I can afford it. My favorite combination. Leaving for Cape May in two weeks for our annual bed and breakfast vacation. I've actually come to look forward to these long weekends at the inn. Nancy R., the innkeeper, and I talk about business, and Bill and I get some uninterrupted time away from telephones. This vacation is one more chance to look back at where I went off track with Patti and what I need to do to return to course.

May 16: Results of the environmental direct mail test are in. We got a whopping 27 percent return! The follow-up calls are generating even more business. This is why I went into business in the first place.

    I just have to stick to what I know best.

May 26: Beginning of vacation. Bill's been talking about taking us to Italy next year. He read an article about renting a villa in Tuscany. A couple we met here this weekend did the same thing last year and encouraged us to do it. Nancy still hasn't sold the inn and won't drop her price. Now she thinks she may want to go to Italy with us. She plans to have the inn sold by next year.

June 1: More than a month without Patti. I am the only one selling and running operations. These are the times when I look back at another detour and wonder what I learned. Did we really need to offer so many different services? Do I really need help in sales? Can the future of the company just ride on my shoulders instead of finding someone to share the load all the time and then being disappointed in the end?

June 4: Not pregnant. Made a decision that keeping us small could hurt me even more than being a big company. I don't want a business that is totally dependent on me. I want to share both the burden and the wealth. I don't need that much. And I don't want to work that hard. The days of working 16 hours are over.

June 5: We are maintaining $12,000 per month in sales and still starving to death. I can't seem to convert proposals into contracts and am not sure what I'm doing wrong. Our average job is now about $3,500 (except for selling mailing lists, which is much lower).

    Time to rework the company around the three things we do well: telemarketing (only certain kinds), fund-raising, and mailing lists.

June 11: The world is a wondrous place. Communism in Russia is coming to an end. Pretty soon we can start marketing to that whole part of the world.

Finally, we got the C—— telemarketing project! They found us through the Yellow Pages at the beginning of the year, and we did a small test for them that was highly successful. Now they want to do a national roll-out. It's a great project and will justify our installing more computers and having a network. I've been wanting to automate our telemarketing area ever since I read about increases in productivity in my trade journals. I also met with staff today to do some fund-raising training. They were all very interested. I think it will help.

June 25: DRM Business Plan for the next five years. My goal is to help businesses around the world to market their goods and services, through a wonderful staff of people who love to make phone calls and do it well, through more efficient, results-oriented two-way communications. In the next five years we will have an automated two-way telecommunications system in place. We will employ smart, articulate people and help them help our clients through excellent training, monitoring, and feedback systems. We will build the company into a multimillion dollar operation.

June 28: Lyn D. and Joe got married back in February; tonight Lyn's mother gave her a beautiful party at the country club. I met Marie, a friend of Lyn's. Marie is out of work and looking for a job. Might be just what we need on a part-time basis. She's done telemarketing, so she understands our business. Plus she has fund-raising experience.

July 3: The day before Independence Day. After looking at our finances for the last year, I conclude that our most profitable business has come from doing particular kinds of telemarketing. What can I do with that? I want us to be this incredible, wonderfully reliable, elegant, dignified telemarketing firm (not like the ones I have visited or seen at some of my client sites). No one seems to treat callers like real people.

July 4: I am rearranging the office, moving all the calling stations out of the back office and into the main area. I need to regard this as our primary service and send that same message to our own employees. To move closer to my goal of being a state-of-the-art, efficient, quality service, I'm also going to computerize every workstation so that we can all be independent and do things more quickly and not send handwritten leads to clients, which is so unprofessional.

July 5: Get a message when I walk in that a vendor has called about an invoice that is 60 days old. Pat gives those to me to deal with. My stomach churns while I return these calls. Sometimes I wait till it is the only message left in my stack unanswered. Then I take a deep breath and dial. The call is never as bad as I anticipated. This vendor and I work out a system. It will be paid off in 60 days.

July 8: To build the telemarketing business, we have to start proactively searching for it. We'll do it the same way we recommend our clients do it: through telemarketing and direct mail.

LESSONS LEARNED

#37: Paying Vendors

Everything I've read about business says always pay your bills on time. But the fact of the matter is, there were many times when I didn't. What I finally learned is that if the vendor is large enough, if you develop a personal relationship with the owner/founder, and if they've been in business longer than you, they remember exactly what you are going through. But it is important to keep talking, keep sending them something. (I once sent $25 on a $5,000 bill and told them I hadn't forgotten and that I personally guaranteed they would get paid. They were.) After 11 years in business, we still work with many of the same vendors we started with. And now I extend credit to newer businesses. Unfortunately, not everyone feels as I do about standing behind a bill. So now I feel that at least I was a good risk. At the time, I woke up a lot in the middle of the night worrying about paying my vendors.

July 17: I had an amazing day. I got the C—— project started. We will need to call 5,000 companies per week for the next 25 weeks. Wow! Everyone is ready and excited.

August 6: Hired Marie to help with the nontelemarketing projects and Len K. to work with telemarketing, both part-time. He responded to our ad in Sunday's classified section. Len will be in sales, with a draw limit of $6,000, but he will also help in the telemarketing department. He has sales experience (he was a copier salesman). This is the first time I've hired a salesperson and told him he could only sell telemarketing services. I am sure I'm on the right track. I'll postpone taking home a bigger check for a while longer.

August 8: Worked with Marie, training her on nontelemarketing project-coordination work. This will free me up to continue selling telemarketing services. She is a quick learner. Then spent an hour with Len K., teaching him about each of our services. Gave him the price list.

August 12: Spent last night with Lyn and her husband, Joe, over dinner. When I called today to thank them, Joe and I got into a conversation about his business. He said that he is wrestling with this whole idea of a laid-back lifestyle where you relax ("golf at a country club and go to a cottage on the weekends") versus working 75 hours per week trying to achieve the American Dream of financial success. How do you walk the fine line between ambition and serenity?

So I'm not the only one struggling with this.

August 18: We are growing. The P—— test was a hit with the client and has resulted in our biggest contract to date, $20,000 per month for the next five months. Janet will be the manager of this project. I have to teach her how to use the computer, and she is petrified. Len and Marie are managing some of the accounts, which frees me up to sell more.

August 28: We need a new computer system, or a new consultant, I'm not sure which. When I got the P—— contract, I decided we should do the whole project on computer, since we had to call more than 125,000 companies. But our sole computer couldn't handle the job. So a client (who found us in the Yellow Pages) who is a computer consultant offered to help us expand our system. But it's a nightmare. Every time three people try to access the next name to make a call, the system freezes. We've replaced the machines, the wiring, and the network software. Personally, I think it's the software, but this consultant assures me that it is not it. We can't get it to work properly, and the job is not going well. I don't know if it's the software, the computer, or the consultant. I feel confused about computers. Do I want too much out of this system? Time to get a second opinion. I'm going to start asking everyone I know who they use to help with computer problems.

August 29: Summer night. A full year since Barb, Lyn, and I sat on my front porch under afghans talking about our dreams. That self-board was a safe place to talk about our uninhibited list of what we wanted out of life. I learned to be clearer about what I wanted from the business, and we trained ourselves to set goals, write them down, and talk about them out loud. We only met for about eight months, but the act of writing down my goals and sharing them out loud has been life-changing. We made the mistake of liking each other so much that we thought we could try a national computer service together. After three or four meetings we realized that it was a terrible idea. We disagreed on almost everything. It almost ruined my relationships with Barb and Lyn. Actually, Barb and Lyn rarely talk to each other anymore as a result of that business idea and those difficult meetings. I'm still not sure why.

August 30: I went back to the office last night to work on a few proposals while no one was using the computers. Brought the dogs with me, and they ran around the office while I worked. When we first moved in, Stan brought his little dog to work, and the tenant above us did the same thing. But the building is slowly filling up, and we may not be able to do this too much longer. The business is getting less casual.

September 6: I've set some pretty lofty goals for the company. I want to hit a million dollars and more in sales. But in looking back, I've decided that I need to concentrate on two things:

1. Stick to one main service.
2. Do good work and work with great employees in a well-ordered environment, and the business will come in.

For me to help Len make $30,000 per year, he needs to bring in $300,000 per year in business. He is getting an $18,000 a year draw and must concentrate strictly on bringing in telemarketing business, where our average sale is $5,000–10,000. He'll also help with customer contact on existing telemarketing projects and count those toward his sales quota to justify his time servicing accounts. I could give him some more of the telemarketing leads that come in for me.

We've been in business for seven years. Every year I've been in business, the phone rings a little more. I wonder what happens after we've been around for 30 years? Is that all business is? Struggle and wait for the phone to ring a little more each year, just because you haven't gone out of business?

I've never arrived at the perfect way to help one of our salespeople to sell as much as me. But it is hard to give new business inquiries to another salesperson when I could turn the lead into business more easily if I handled it myself. While Len is new, I'm still following up on the leads until they are close to becoming contracts; then I bring him into it.

September 6: Having a problem with Marie, Lyn's friend who is helping us out in the office. She always seems to be on the verge of losing her temper. She is not well liked by the other employees, and she is just on the edge of being rude with customers. I have to do a better job of finding people. I also have to:

1. Stop writing most of the proposals—Len should be doing them all. But I am doing most of them.
2. Stop making all the final presentations to clients. I don't feel comfortable letting Len finalize the bigger projects when he gets close, because I'm afraid we'll lose it and we can't afford to lose anything right now.
3. Get everyone in the office comfortable with operating the computers. Len is still doing everything in longhand. I actually caught him trying to give a client a handwritten proposal!

September 19: We finally got a new computer consultant (thanks to a new client who loaned us her consultant) and new software that I read about in one of my trade journals. No more software written for me by consultants. I'm sticking to off-the-shelf stuff. The project is going well now.

September 20: My deal with Len is that he gets a minor commission if he works on any account, even if I bring it in. That frees me up to go out and get more business. I'm not sure this is working, because Janet was the manager and now in a way she is reporting to Len. It's also hard to keep everyone informed of what's going on, since I'm still out of the office a lot.

October 19: Had tea and sandwiches with Doug H., who had been my client at the environmental company (he left a few months ago when the owner had a stroke and they closed the company). Now he's teaching business at a local college. We talked about business long enough for me to get really angry with myself and Doug. I told Doug that I was happy maintaining the status quo, enjoying what we have, concentrating on our customers.

Doug says if you are not growing, you are falling behind, and eventually your competition will take over. Is it time to run the company more seriously? With a formal vision and goals? Is it possible to do that and have a beautiful life?

November 5: Marie is gone. She resigned, thank goodness. Got another job and thanked me for giving her a job when she needed one. But damage to the company from turnaround like this is hard to measure. What is the cost to clients of having to deal each time with someone new who doesn't know them or their project?

December 8: Meeting with Barb M. at the V. Hotel. We had agreed to spend an overnight session together, planning our goals for the year as we did last year with Lyn. We rented a large room and brought our juice, fruit, cookies, and goals lists. Lyn was not with us. Barb and Lyn don't talk anymore, ever since we tried launching a business idea together. Not a falling out exactly, but uncomfortable.

LESSONS LEARNED

#38: The Cause and Effect of Turnover

There are probably studies on this subject. In my business, turnover cost me plenty. Turnover caused more mistakes and took more staff time for training, and problems escalated due to inexperience. But turnover was also caused every time I changed direction. The employee skills I needed in one year weren't required the following year because our company was providing a different service. So every time I started a new service, I usually had to hire another new employee.

I hate to admit it, but it always comes back to the vision and focus of the owner. Had I concentrated on a single service and built the company around it, we'd probably still have many of the employees I started with in my first year in business. And think of how experienced they would be right now.

I also realize that people left because we were not successful and therefore couldn't pay benefits or competitive salaries. Again, it comes back to the owner. If I had concentrated on a single service and built it profitably, I could have afforded better wages and benefits.

December 9: The next morning. As usual, when Barb and I get together, the room looks as if a bomb hit it. But we got our goals on paper and will send each other copies this week.

Barb suggested I talk to her counselor at SCORE (Senior Core of Retired Executives), sponsored by the Small Business Administration. She said that Edwin B., one of the counselors, could help me develop a serious business plan and determine my role in the company. Two other goals: Look for a weekend cottage, and try getting back into writing for publication again. Send out at least two letters to editors suggesting story ideas that relate to the business, since it is my favorite subject.

January 3: A new year. The months stretch out like 12 journeys, 12 trips waiting to be taken. I want a stable, profitable company. I want to be able to afford a bigger paycheck. I want to find a weekend cottage. I want to have a family.

January 15: Got a call from George S. He was one of the men I talked to, who had a direct mail business in Cleveland that his dad had started. He had been getting my newsletters for the last seven years and decided to give me a call and see how I was doing. He wants to figure out a way for us to work together. He is changing the way he does business, has eliminated all his salespeople, and is looking for distributors. Wants to know if we can sell his services in our city. I ask him to send his material.

February 7: In analyzing our income and expenses from last year (we hit $260,000 in sales), I see that we really have to put our focus on telemarketing. This is it. I have to concentrate on where our best chances for income are located.

February 17: I'm more sure than ever that self-actualization starts when the basic human needs are met. That means you are able to pay your bills without stress. Alexandra Stoddard's books about living beautifully don't make sense unless you feel you can pay all of your bills and you are comfortable with your basic needs: food, shelter, and clothing (or payroll, expenses, and a reasonable pay-check). I know that I'm just now rising above that.

On self-actualization in business: It's easier to think win/win or no-deal in business when you don't need the deal to eat.

March 1: Ginny C., a client, asks me to review her fund-raising pro-ject and wants me to meet Rick M., a colleague of hers who will be helping us with the spring campaign. He and I hit it off right away. He runs a telemarketing fund-raising office for a local university and has volunteered his help with our campaign.

March 25: Bought a used book at the library called *How to Live Life on 24 Hours a Day*. The book—from 1908—says that most people center their lives around work. They waste their lives getting ready for it, traveling to it, doing it, thinking about it afterwards, relaxing at home to recover from it, and then going to bed to get ready for it the next day. Hmmm. So he recommends: Sleep less, wake up early to pursue important projects like studying music or literature, develop other interests such as gardening, journal writ-ing, history, art, painting. Okay, so not much has changed. I think he's right.

March 26: Our office looks brand new! We've been doing so much telemarketing that I had Barbara Ma.'s brother, Fred (she's one of my telemarketers), build us beautiful custom-made desks that are larger than the average telemarketing workstation (for more comfort) but smaller than a standard desk. They are a beautiful shade of purple.

We are still holding regular staff meetings, and I still get numbers from each department.

Pat and Janet have been doing a terrific job. But Len's sales numbers have not exceeded $5,000 per month, and he's been here for eight months. I had agreed to expect only $12,000 in sales from him per month, since half his time was devoted to helping Janet run the telemarketing area. So he's on probation. We're going to watch his numbers closely for the next few months. Also, Janet and Len fight a lot (like a mismatched married couple—it's so annoying because they don't even know they are doing it).

End of Year Seven

Year Eight

Executive Summary

Primary services:	Telemarketing and direct mail
Number of employees:	20 (mostly part-time telemarketers)
Business location:	1,500 square feet in converted elementary school
Sources of new business:	Networking, Yellow Pages, referrals, word of mouth, networking
Financing:	No new capital
Average monthly sales:	$40,000
Average sale:	$5,000
Annual sales:	Approx. $480,000
Greatest challenge:	Starting over again with a modified vision of the business
Comments:	Patti is gone. I return the business to our primary services, telemarketing and direct mail, and we are rewarded (I feel) by the largest contract to date, worth more than $100,000. We're also bidding on more large contracts without fear of the size of these proposals because I finally feel our telemarketing service is effective and we can prove that it works.

April 2: The seventh anniversary of DRM passed quietly yesterday. I'm turning 35 in a few weeks. I want us to have this business at least for the next 60 years (assuming I live to be 95).

Portions of this section are reprinted with permission from *Inc.* magazine.

April 5: Notes from meeting with Jan R. She was a client, but we have become personal friends. She has gotten into general business coaching, especially for women business owners. We've been meeting in my office for about two hours every few months. I'm paying her $50 an hour for access to an objective ear. It is hard talking openly to other employees or friends. Bill, my husband, is great, but I can't talk intensely about business issues for too long with him.

Jan feels we would be more successful if we ran the office more professionally (e.g., answering the phone on the second ring, and improving the look of our client reports and even our invoices). She also feels that we need to pay our employees more and find an experienced salesperson who knows our industry. She feels Len is from the old school of selling, and he admits he hates the computers. She agrees that the computers will also help us attract bigger, better-paying clients. She feels we need someone who is more progressive to represent us. What I don't tell her is that most of her ideas cost money that we don't really have.

April 13: We need more computers to grow, but I can't afford them. I have to go into debt if I want them that badly. I am taking the company in an expensive new direction. If we make a commitment to concentrate in this area of marketing (automated telemarketing) and I am wrong again, I won't be able to bear it.

May 1: As much as I love this business, there is a part of me that wonders if this is all there is. Worrying all the time, struggling with staff, worrying about getting sick, meeting payroll, solving problems. I'm not sure I'm making enough money out of all this to justify this pressure.

May 4: Problems with the C—— project. To honor the contract and finish the project on time, we must call a certain number of businesses per week. We estimated the payroll needed to meet that goal, but the callers aren't able to reach as many businesses as we projected. Janet says we have to increase staff. I say they need to be more efficient. Len says it's the computer system that is too slow. They are still at each other's throats on most issues. So who do I believe? Them or me?

May 5: I'm learning that pure quiet time is the only thing that calms me, helps me to think. Thank goodness for weekends. It's Sunday night, and we sit on the front porch for dinner. The garden looks pristine, the tulips are in bloom, and the beds are weeded. A gentle spring rain starts. We keep the stereo playing and sit outside wrapped in sweaters watching the rain. Can life be bad with nights like this?

When I'm having a bad time at work, I wonder what it would be like to not work. Just stay at home, live on less. I always think this way when cash is tight and we are about to take on more risk.

May 6: An incredible day. We are exploding at the seams with phone work, mail work, research work (George A., my public speaking teacher, has given us some work through his research firm because we have experience in telephone surveys through our telemarketing division). Also, the phone continues to ring with people inquiring about our services.

May 7: I meet with Rick M. about Ginny C.'s project, and we talk about our industry. I invite Rick M. to see our offices. He gives me a few referrals.

May 8: Had our first quarterly staff meeting. This is in addition to our weekly manager meetings and is part of my plan to share more of the responsibility with all employees in the company. I gathered everyone into the calling area (no place else was big enough) and we sat around introducing ourselves and telling each other some personal things about ourselves. Then I talked about the first three months of the year and what's coming up between now and the end of June. It was a way for the callers to hear what was going on instead of relying on Janet to tell them. I also started a little two-page newsletter that Pat hands out with the paychecks. I try to mention everyone in the company at least once.

June 10: Goals meeting. Barb and I have been meeting again every few months. But it hasn't been the same without Lyn. For some reason, the third person maintains a more formal process. With the two of us, it's just two old friends talking. So Barb invited Stephanie S. to join us. Today the three of us meet for the first time.

Barb and I have been open with each other for two and half years now. Steph finds it hard to be completely open. That's okay; I don't need to share in quite the same way anymore.

The goal I talk about at the meeting is my intent to share the company more. Pat pays the bills but doesn't really understand where the money comes from. Janet works on projects but doesn't really understand the impact when her staff makes a mistake. Len brings in contracts but doesn't truly take responsibility for bringing in his monthly quota. He doesn't worry that I won't be able to pay the bills. Well, no one worries about that except me.

June 18: Met with George S. from Cleveland again about promoting his direct mail services, and I tell him about our telemarketing services. He now has about four distributors lined up and says he's glad he made the change. He is putting together a major seminar for all clients and distributors, and he invites me to Cleveland in a few months.

June 19: I have been meeting on and off with Ed B., my SCORE counselor. But he's not rushing me on the business plan. He says whenever I finish the next draft to call him and we'll get together. Like most things in this business, I am the core. No one is going to stand over me telling me what to do. And that, after all, is what I wanted. But the business plan sits unfinished after six months of playing around and about four meetings with Ed. I need to move ahead and then use the plan to get a loan so that I can buy 12 more computers. Time to stop being so scared. Time to commit to this business and my customers. From reading and working on this plan, I realize how unfocused I have been. Ed actually was the one who pointed it out to me. As an observer and an experienced businessman, he looked at my general description of the business and said he couldn't understand it. If he can't, the bank can't. If the bank can't, maybe our customers can't.

He also strongly advises that we need to move from keeping our financial records on greenbar ledger pads to a computer program. I have been avoiding the subject with Pat because I know computers make her very nervous.

June 28: Bill and I are going to Italy next June. We read an article in a travel magazine about two families who rented a villa in Tuscany with a swimming pool. We can probably find some friends to share the expense with us. We're going to work on it together.

July 13: Bought Peachtree accounting software at the mall last night. Took it into Pat. We are going to put it on the computer this summer so that I can turn financial records into the bank from Peachtree. She asks if she has to do this in addition to all her other work. I say yes and assure Pat I will help her.

July 14: Sometimes I think the world is divided into two groups of people: those who go through life looking for pain (anxiety, jealousy, fear, procrastination, negativity, complication on the side of pain) and those who don't. I am in the first group, and I am tired of it. There is this door, and on the other side is hope, love, courage, beauty, joy, order, action, simplicity, positive feelings. Where is the damn key?

July 26: Len is gone. He hit his $6,000 draw limit and decided he couldn't afford to stay on straight commission. This time, there was no anger, as there was with Patti. And because Janet has no one to fight with, the office is blessedly quiet. But I am no further ahead than when Patti left. I still have not figured out what it takes to keep salespeople.

I promoted Rod and Bud (both callers and friends who went to school together) into sales from the telemarketing department. Both have proved their ability to make cold calls and generate appointments, both are bright college graduates who are comfortable with computers. I'm training them to sell. I wanted us to grow 20 percent this year, and right now we're running at 25 percent of last year. They are paid 25 percent salary, 75 percent commission.

As part of their training, I send them to George S.'s seminar in Cleveland. When I talk to George at the end of the day, he is disappointed that I didn't come myself. I apologize and ask him if he spent any time with Rod and Bud. He is quiet and I can tell he doesn't want to share his opinion. Keep an eye on them, he says. They are very young.

July 27: I am determined to find a cottage by a lake that we can afford. Bill and I start taking Sunday drives looking at property and cottages within a three-hour drive of the house.

July 28: Last night I did an assessment of our eight years in business. Starting from scratch, over the last eight years we have generated more than $1.5 million in sales. That is an amazing number. Unfortunately, I spent it all.

July 29: When I finally sit down with Rod and Bud to talk about their trip to Cleveland, they turn in their receipts. I made the mistake of not giving them a limit on expenses. They stayed in a $100 per night hotel. Tight-rein time.

August 15: The C—— project will be coming to an end next week, and we have nothing to replace it with. I've been spending less time selling and more time helping Rod and Bud to sell. So I can see a hole in the schedule in two weeks. Not enough work. We may have to lay off people if I can't bring in some accounts or if Rod and Bud can't bring something in. They are so casual. I'm not sure they see the seriousness of this situation.

I'm frustrated with Pat too. She still hasn't gotten Peachtree working on the computer. I installed the software, read the manual, and figured out what had to be entered and showed her how to enter clients and vendors, but she hasn't gotten to it. I hired a temp to help with our computer work. He's great, but he doesn't know Peachtree.

I get so angry sometimes when my employees are floundering. They look to me to save them, tell them what to do. And I look at them thinking, why? Why should I, working as hard as I am, save you? I figured it out for myself. Why don't you figure it out for yourself?

I think I would be more patient if I could figure out how to consistently bring in new business through someone other than me. We do lots of short-term projects. We need a steady flow of new ones every month to protect us and the company. I need to start redesigning our services. I need to find ways to serve our clients on a long-term basis. Just not sure how.

August 17: Finished the business plan with Ed B. from SCORE. My father helped me with some of the charts and graphs on his computer at home and mailed them to me. John S., our accountant, had all our financial records and gave us the financial sections we needed. Nothing ready from Peachtree. Then I set up meetings with two banks. Ed B. said if I was going to write a serious business plan, I might as well ask for serious money. He said most banks won't take you seriously if you don't ask for $100,000. We don't need $100,000, and I don't think we are doing enough business right now to justify it. But we will. So I'm asking for a $75,000 line of credit so that I don't have to lose sleep over payroll if the receivables are there to cover it. And I need a $28,000 loan to buy the additional computers to automate the telemarketing area and train everyone. I should hear from both banks in the next two weeks.

I also talked to Ed about Rod and Bud. They are just not producing. Ed asks me if I have set up monthly sales quotas that we review together. No. I've never done that, I admit. Ed was a sales manager for a company and scolds me for not doing it sooner. Together we figure out that the minimum they can bring in is $15,000 per month to keep their jobs. I come back to the office and sit down with them. I tell them they have three months to attain that level of sales. They agree.

August 22: Met Larry L., a salesperson for a telephone equipment manufacturer. I had agreed to see him because of a telemarketing call that I received about our equipment. He's trying to sell me a new telephone system, and he also told me his company is looking for a new telemarketing company to help them generate more leads for their sales force. He tells me who to call.

August 24: Barb M. tells me about a new networking group for women business owners that's starting. The group nearest me meets at a restaurant less than half a mile from the office. I decide to attend the September meeting.

August 26: Our first company picnic was a big success. Everyone brought food from home, and we sat at the picnic table on the grass next to my office door and played Parcheesi while the phone sat 20 feet from us on a really long extension cord. We were also celebrating the end of the P—— project. We did meet the deadline, and the callers did help me by increasing their productivity. But while we sit and play games, I worry. We don't have business to replace this project. Downhill again. We seem to go through these cycles, expanding and contracting. When we are busy I slow down. When the business slows down, I speed up. There has to be another way.

September 2: I've decided to submit an application for an advisory board to an organization called PowerLink. Barb M. called me four or five times in the last month and said they are looking for companies that are growing. I didn't correct her. It is true that in our first year we did $27,000 and last year we did a little more than $250,000. I suppose I should feel proud of the accomplishment. But as the years pass, the longer I am in business, the more I question my own ability to grow this company single-handedly.

How does a company grow from $50,000 in sales to $10 million or $100 million? Am I doing something wrong? I am willing to stretch to find out, even if it means adding another set of tasks to a very full schedule. [Note: In my speaking to women's business groups, my favorite metaphor of the business owner is the man on *The Ed Sullivan Show* who balanced spinning dinner plates on the ends of tall sticks. Just as he had 15 spinning, one would start to wobble and then another and then another. This PowerLink advisory board seems like adding seven more plates.]

September 10: First Women's Business Network meeting at a nearby restaurant. There are eight women; most work from their homes. But as we go around the table sharing our backgrounds and why we are in business, I can see clearly that we all want more control over our lives and that no one at the table is making any money to speak of. But I decide to join and put the dates in my organizer for the next year.

September 16: The first bank (the one where Bill and I bank) turned me down without any real explanation. I know my financial statements aren't strong enough. Still waiting to hear from the bank where we keep our business checking and payroll accounts.

September 17: Jim S., from the second bank (where we have our business checking account), called to set up a meeting. We got the loan ($25,000) to buy the computers and a $55,000 line of credit! Hurray!

September 18: I drove past Bill K.'s office after meeting with the bank and stopped in to say hello. He is smiling again. His old account stopped working with the downtown ad agency after getting some of their bills. In the meantime, he never did replace them.

He admitted that he was always terrible at sales. He was about to get a job, when the client came back to him. I drive back to the office thoughtful. I wouldn't have to do that. I feel as if I could go out tomorrow and replace anything I lost today. And that is what I will do now, to replace the C—— account. I don't think I could work for anyone ever again, except my clients, and my employees.

September 19: I hired Ruth Ann, an assistant for Janet, since Len is gone and she has no backup if she's sick or on vacation. Within a week Janet asks for three months off without pay for personal reasons. So here we are with a brand new manager. But Ruth Ann has been a loyal caller and ran the place where she worked before. Since the C—— project is over, there aren't as many people to manage. No time to train Ruth, but she's been around for a while. She's doing great.

September 20: I think we found a cottage. It is well within our budget and is completely furnished. We're going to go back and look at it again in a few weeks and then make an offer. We're going to put down enough that our mortgage will be so low we can afford to pay it no matter what happens to the business.

September 22: We got the telephone equipment telemarketing contract! It happened that fast. I still can't believe it. It will replace the P—— job in hours. This is the largest single contract we've ever gotten. I've designed it to be for six months with an option to renew for another 12 months. And all because I took a sales call and ended up having a great conversation with the salesperson.

October 1: I've been selected as one of two companies in the PowerLink program. The other company is owned by Andrea F., another of Barb M.'s friends. Barb would help set the pace for this experiment. They want to start small and get input from the business owners so that subsequent "classes" will benefit. I am thrilled and inform my employees of our selection. Their response is reserved.

October 2: Steph, Barb, and I had our self-board meeting. I admitted that I need to be a better salesperson and Steph suggested I take some sales training classes. But when?

[Note: I think I have to keep going after large, national accounts.]

October 3: Hired Rob M. to help me with customer service, especially on this new account. Clients have to wait a whole day for me to get back to them, since I'm out so much. And with Len and Janet gone and Ruth Ann being new in Janet's job as an interim manager, we don't have a lot of coverage in the office when clients call. Rob is going to talk to clients and make sure all jobs are going smoothly. It's a new position, but I need someone to watch over the jobs when I'm not there and this seems like the answer. He's the brother-in-law of one our employees and approached me about a job.

October 15: We are starting the A—— telemarketing contract. It lasts for six months, and then we will evaluate it. It will be telephone lead generation, which we know how to do very well. We are going to hire a few more callers, this time full-time. And we're finally going to start offering health insurance if an employee works at least 26 hours per week. This is the way I'm going to keep good callers, I believe. We'll see what happens.

October 26: Bill called about the cottage. Our offer was accepted. We could be in it by the end of the year.

November 1: Hired a new telemarketer, Diane N., who has previous experience as a salesperson. I'm going to wait until the end of the year. If she's still around and doing well, she might be a good person to help me.

November 15: I got a call from Kara A., who works with PowerLink as a volunteer and will be my contact through this whole PowerLink board year. She's sending me the list and resumes of the board members who have been picked for me. I accept them all, knowing that Barb M. has been involved with picking them for me and she's always been someone a few years ahead of me in this world of business. The board is made up of

> Michael P., owner and founder of a multimillion dollar
>   metals brokerage business

Steve M., marketing director of the city symphony

Brian M., an associate with a large accounting firm, which is one of the sponsors of this PowerLink organization

Sarah K., a quality control specialist with a large manufacturing company

Susan W., founder and owner of a $500,000 computer consulting business

November 18: Continuing problems with Pat. She seems to be frozen over this Peachtree project. And now the pending board of directors meetings have her nervous. She has always just done exactly what I asked her. I can see that we are headed in a direction that will require more accountability from her, and I may have raised the bar a notch too high. Maybe the holidays will calm her down.

November 23: Met with Rod and Bud separately. Neither one has brought in a single account in months. They just are too young and too immature and have no sense of urgency or drive whatsoever. I wish them well and swear, as I do every time, that I will learn from this experience.

December 24: When we get home from church, we get a message on the answering machine that our mortgage for the cottage has been approved and we will receive the agreement in the mail next week. I am elated. Another goal met. Maybe it is the beginning of more good things.

December 30: I talk to Diane N. She did great on all the telemarketing projects that Ruth Ann gave her. She's in her late forties and has a ton of experience in sales and management. She says the owner of her apartment building worked at a telemarketing company and she sees this as a new industry she'd like to learn more about. I offer her a sales position with a $20,000 draw plus commission. She accepts easily. We'll do some training after the holidays. Her title will be sales manager.

January 1: New Year's Day. As I rewrite my goals for the year, the publishing goal comes up again. I never did send any inquires to editors. Maybe this PowerLink experience is worth a letter to George G., the editor in chief at *Inc.* magazine. I've been reading it since the year before I started the business. Sometimes I think he couldn't possibly identify with companies our size. But he seems approachable.

January 2: I receive the list of five board members who were selected for me. I approve them and add two of my own. I pick Dwight F. because he has been a client since 1984 and watched us shift from being a consulting firm to becoming a service bureau. Rick M. has extensive telemarketing experience, more than anyone else on the board, and he is a prospective client.

January 5: Draft three major goals from the list of 75 we came up with at our annual company meeting: Hit $750,000 in sales; analyze and improve internal communications and systems that have an impact on customer service; analyze my management methods; figure out how to delegate better and help grow the company in a responsible way.

I am unsure of what to tell the board about the company. I wish I could pay my employees better. I wish we could be 100 percent error-free on every client project. I still let receivables slip over 60 days. I still lose money on some jobs because we hire a new person who makes a mistake, so we do the work over again. We never seem to have enough cash. I still don't have my accounting on the computer. And when I go away for long weekends, I still check in once, sometimes twice, a day, assuming that my help is needed with a problem at work.

January 15: We close the year at $367,422. That's almost a 37 percent increase over last year, despite the flat economy. My decision to shift our resources to automate our telemarketing service seems to have been a good one. It means we can accept work from larger companies that need fast turnarounds. It also means I have more employees to manage and a $25,000 loan to repay (a few more plates to juggle). We are cash hungry all the time, and we have more debt than I've ever exposed us to. And, yes, the Jeep has 93,000 miles on it.

January 21: I attend my Women's Business Network meeting to tell them about my selection as one of the companies to receive an advisory board of directors.

In this group, I own one of the largest companies. Though we never discuss gross sales (do men do that?), I know that of 15 women at my meetings three of us have employees paid "over" the table. The rest are home-based.

January 26: We go to the cottage immediately after the closing and spend the weekend. There are 12 inches of snow on the ground, which is no problem for the Jeep. I feel no matter what happens to the business, the cottage is something else that is my reward for all the hard work.

January 28: Pat gives her notice. Company getting too big. She asks me to let her move aside so that I can hire someone with more accounting and finance skills. I agree, though not happily. She and I have worked together since the beginning, and it devastates me that she is leaving. She is the organizer, the one who knows what I'm thinking before I open my mouth. When I'm out of the office, she runs it, pays the bills, does the payroll. I trust her without blinking. I cannot even imagine what to do next. Yet, I will not mention this to the board. Instead, I concentrate on major goals.

A part-time employee who is majoring in accounting approaches me after Pat's announcement to let me know he is interested in her position. He feels we really need someone with a bachelor's degree in finance. I agree to let him start doing some bookkeeping work in the evenings.

February 4: First board meeting. Three of seven board members attend. The rest called in their excuses. I am reluctant to go ahead but don't want to inconvenience the three who have made time to attend. We decide to set up a second meeting for the other four for a few weeks later and proceed. Presentations by three of my managers and me. Nervous!

Each board member feels compelled to share in the advice giving. I furiously take notes. Eliminate employee presentations. Employees are too concerned with operations. The board is more concerned with the big picture. Since they are giving me only eight hours (two hours for each quarterly meeting this year), anything extraneous just takes up valuable time.

Brian M. says I don't talk enough about the finances of the business. Mike P. agrees. "A company with weak financial controls is a weak company," Mike says. I am asked if I have ever done a cash flow analysis. I say no. Brian offers to show me how, and we set up a meeting for three weeks later. [Note: We will reschedule that meeting three times. Eventually, Brian changes jobs and leaves the board. This was his only meeting.]

Mike says I should be doing something called teleselling—selling my client's products directly over the phone—like a friend of his who owns a telemarketing company in Pittsburgh. It means long-term contracts, something we have few of. Most of our work is on a project basis, which Mike thinks saps my company's stability. We specialize in telemarketing on special projects lasting four to 12 weeks—usually lead-generation projects for manufacturing companies. He notes that a long-term contract with an international manufacturer is part of what helped him build sales in his own company.

I have many ideas about how to build the company's sales. That isn't one of them. I write it down but don't actively pursue the suggestion any further. After all, I rationalize, only a few telemarketing companies in the tri-state area offer the level of professional service that we do. How can we turn down the small-project work that has built the company?

Still, the long-term notion of Mike's suggestion is a good one. In the next few months I will be renegotiating with A—— and will ask for a revised 12-month agreement with a possible extension for up to three years.

Steve M. asks if I use anybody else for advice besides the advisory board. I tell him I really haven't used anyone other than consultants to help me solve specific problems. We paid computer consultants to help us when we made the investment to automate the telemarketing department. I also hired Jan R., who helped us look at how we delivered services and refine our customer service skills.

Steve says my limited use of outside counsel is a mistake. I need to cultivate relationships with my banker, my accountant, and my attorney. I take notes but wonder how much all that cultivation will cost me in extra billings.

I do, however, add all the people he named, plus three of my regular consultants, to my advisory board memo list. Following the meeting I will send the board an update on company activities and will send the exact same materials to those additional six people. [Note: Jim S., my banker, after receiving the material, called immediately to thank me and has given me a lead for business at the bank. My accountant, John S., started giving me extra hours of attention at no charge. I also notice I am not wasting time playing "catch-up" with them. They appear to be reading everything I send them. Amazing.]

Mike P.: "Always remember this and write it down somewhere." He pauses while I pull out my pen. "Strategy first, structure second." I ask him to clarify. "Figure out where you want to go. Then work on logistics." I am being told in a nice way to stop pressing so hard against the daily tasks.

What is my long-term vision? What is the role I want to play? Those questions keep popping up, and I do not want to deal with them. My way of doing business is the one my father taught me—get up every day and just work hard.

March 1: I write a letter to George G. at *Inc.* to see if he'd be interested in publishing my diary entries about this PowerLink board. I send it to Barb M. and her PowerLink group to make sure it's okay with them. They tell me to go ahead.

March 15: I finish the final paperwork to incorporate the business. This board makes me feel that we are entering a new phase of the company. It is time for me to take it seriously, too. Mike M., an attorney friend who has been borrowing my computer at night, offers to do the filing. I have Ken J., who is my regular attorney with a large firm in town, but I agree.

March 17: When Mike P. talks about anything, I find myself listening especially closely. He has a service business with employees. He is experienced in the art of business ownership. Most of my other board members are not owners. I invite him to lunch. I come to the meeting with an advisory board file one-inch thick and an organizer stuffed so full of notes that it no longer zippers shut. Mike walks in with a calendar/phone directory the size of a small calculator in his breast pocket. He has built his company to $10 million in revenues. I closed the year at billings of $367,000. Was I bogging myself down in paperwork and missing the point? He reminds me again that I need to install daily and weekly financial controls. He also gives me the name of his health insurance administrator.

March 23: At 6:30 tonight, George G. of *Inc.* called me personally. I was still at work, of course, and we talked for almost an hour. He told me to keep the journal and send him pages. I told him I'd send him a group of diary entries sometime in September. Another goal met. Is it really this easy?

March 30: Ken J., my regular attorney, contacts me. He has seen the incorporation advertisement and wants to know if he has done something to offend me. We agree to meet for lunch at his club. I tell him what is going on with the business and about our new PowerLink board. He admits he could be more useful to the company if we saw each other on a regular basis. He sets up quarterly lunches at his club to discuss the business.

April 1: DRM Inc. is eight years old. Don't want to think about it.

End of Year Eight

Year Nine

Executive Summary

Primary Services:	Telemarketing services
Number of employees:	30
Business location:	Same as Year Eight
Sources of new business:	Networking, referrals, directory advertising, memberships in organizations
Capital resources:	Bank issued line of credit and $25,000 bank-issued equipment loan
Average monthly sales:	$45,000
Average sales:	$5,000
Annual sales:	Approx. $550,000
Major challenge:	Revealing my biggest fear: that I didn't have a clue as to how to make this business successful
Comments:	This was the turning-point year. I was frustrated enough that I even considered getting out of the business entirely. It was the commitment to work with the PowerLink board that convinced me to keep going.

April 3: We almost miss payroll. Our largest client (representing about 30 percent of our monthly billings) changed the criteria for what constitutes a lead—and we are being paid by the lead. As a result we've been turning in one lead every five hours instead of every hour. Losing about $500 a day.

I know we will run out of all cash reserves in the next two weeks, and our receivables are below adequate levels. (I've always used the shorthand version of a current ratio, adding up all of my bills and mak-

Portions of this section are reprinted with permission from *Inc.* magazine.

ing sure they come to less than 33 percent of my outstanding receivables.) I quickly write out a list of things I will have to do to stem the losses. I know we are going to have to lay off staff, and that is probably Plan B. Plan C is to renegotiate the contract.

April 7: Second board meeting. This time five of seven attend. The meeting moves slowly. Instead of talking about payroll, I say vaguely that we are squeezed "a little" for cash.

One of them asks if I have a line of credit. I do, I tell them. Then you are okay, they say. I wonder to myself how that makes sense. Yes, I have the line as security, but accessing it only gives me another debt to pay with receivables I don't have right now. I hope someone asks me the right questions, but no one does.

And I still feel unfamiliar with these people. Nothing in the notes from PowerLink has prepared me for corporate executives who seem to think I am doing okay. It is Mike P. who asks if he can help with financials and brings a small piece of paper with ideas he wants to share with me about business.

The meeting ends as the first one did. I have a list of new pieces of advice to hold under the light and decide if they make sense or if I should throw them out.

April 17: Financial controls still out of whack. My young accounting major/bookkeeper is up to 30 hours a week on nights and weekends. He is not able to give me regular weekly reports on time, let alone the ones Mike P. recommended. I try to understand why this is so difficult. I realize that our systems were purely dependent on a single person, Pat, who was organized and set up her own system. It's a hard one for my bookkeeper to follow, and I am not around much to supervise him. We lose valuable time while he learns on the job—typical in a tiny company. But the impact of losing one person in our small office has been great.

Seems like another catch-22. Not big enough to hire backup for every position. Everyone straining to get everything done in a day. Who has time to write a procedures manual? I wonder again, How the hell does a multimillion dollar company get that way?

I review contracts and personnel with Ruth Ann, the telemarketing supervisor, and Diane, my new sales manager. We agree that

---

LESSONS LEARNED

#39: Hiring the Next Person in Line

In more than one instance, I made hasty hiring decisions because we were so understaffed. If one person left, they usually did two or three jobs. I seemed to hire anyone who fell into my radius within a few days of the open position being created. Looking back, I realize that if I had simply forced myself to put an ad in the Sunday newspaper, I probably could have had a *choice* of more experienced people. But I never thought I had the luxury of time. In retrospect, I spent a fortune hiring the closest candidate rather than the most qualified.

---

while we work on resolving problems with our major contract, we must lay off six people.

April 21: I cancel meeting with Brian M. after being off for four days and coming back to find office out of control. Operations problems with our major account still setting us back.

Payables backed to 90 days. The money I borrowed last year seems crushing now that our major account is generating 20 percent of its normal billings. Our meeting to present the account with a new plan is next week. Though all our other projects are going well, I can't see it. These are the times when I'd like to walk away from the whole business, chalk up my debts, work out payback arrangements, and go work at Wal-Mart as a cashier. I call these my "depth-of-despair days."

April 22: Second D-of-D day in a row. I wonder why I put myself through this. I could be a corporate executive again with a paid staff and someone else worrying about the bills. I feel if I have one more day of settling disputes between employees, no matter how minor, I will shake them until their heads rattle.

April 23: I meet with Steve M. He said he would help any way he could but could not attend the April meeting. We meet for 45 minutes in his office to talk about DRM's marketing. Instead we talk about salespeople. I tell him about the nine I have employed in eight years. My tendency in the early years was to hire inexperienced people.

I tell him about my latest hire. Diane N. is the exception. She came to us as a mid-level manager laid off from a larger firm. She needed a job and wanted to try telemarketing. I moved her into sales within eight weeks of working with her. But I see that she is also good at helping me look at operations. She is interested in how her clients can be best served, so we spend hours talking about how to do that.

I also admit to Steve that I love sales, love being outside, and truly dislike the day-to-day grind of operations. At the point where a project is set up and running smoothly, I am restless and anxious to be on the move again.

Steve asks if I had made those sales hiring decisions alone. Again, this advice issue. Of course I made them alone. Who else was there to negotiate salary etc? He suggests that in the future I never hire a salesperson or manager without letting two or three people inside the company or board members help with interviewing.

Whenever I have discussions about my hiring decisions with people who work for bigger companies, my internal reaction is usually the same: Have you ever given up a part of your own salary to hire someone in your department? But I do feel Steve's ideas are valid for the most part and add them to the notebook of suggestions I have been carrying around.

He also points out that we have no long-term marketing strategy. Here we go again. He feels my fears about entering certain markets are unfounded. I could always raise capital if I needed it to fund the launch of a new division. To a longtime bootstrapper like me, these are foreign words. I've never made capital investments without contracts in hand. Is that my mistake? Is that why we aren't doing better? Am I too cautious? Too afraid to borrow investment capital to expand the business? My computer loan still looms over me. The thought of borrowing again before paying that loan off seems out of the question.

April 24: New contract agreed to with A ———. We will begin new program next week.

April 27: Must fire Rob M. He was a great employee but has a nasty temper, which flared with employees and clients. I had issued a written warning in March without the board's advice. Tonight, while I prepare what I am going to say to this man, I heed Steve M.'s advice and call a board member with personnel experience. Rick M. listens and assures me I am doing the right thing. Then he gives me the words to say. I write them on the back of an envelope in my kitchen as he dictates.

I feel better after talking to him. Then call George S. Not a board member but someone I have shared business problems and advice with on and off ever since I started working with the board.

It is strange, this idea of asking others for input. Almost like learning a new language. I keep referring to my flash cards. I am also discovering how willing people are to share their own business problems.

George admits that after running his business for 15 years, he felt he had made terrible hiring decisions for the first 10 years! What does he do differently now? Watches more closely during a 90-day probation and gets feedback from other employees before making a decision to hire a person permanently after the probation. He says when he started asking his employees for advice, they started telling him things about employees that they had kept under their hats. They thought George knew what was going on and chose to ignore it. I have employees who have accused me of doing the same thing.

Interesting idea. I've never asked any employees for their opinions before taking someone off probation. In this employee's case, I could have saved myself four months of headaches and maybe an unemployment arbitration hearing.

May 15: Phone consultation with Jan R. If I add her to the list, I am now getting advice on the way the company is organized from my sales manager, Diane N.; my advisory board; and seven outside consultants (15 plates in the air!).

Jan is almost impatient when she reminds me I still have not consulted with another, larger telemarketing firm (we are now doing 80 percent telemarketing) to see how larger firms are structured.

After our phone call I immediately call Chris H., a woman who works for an acquaintance who owns a huge telemarketing company in Philadelphia. I have been meaning to do this for months, and something always seemed to get in the way. I ask her if she can come in and help me look at operations. She agrees enthusiastically.

May 22: Chris H. arrives right on time, at 8:30 A.M. We talk for almost three hours. As I furiously take notes, I realize how important she has been in helping with the growth of her company. The owner, Jim R., is a salesman; Chris is an organizer. She is neat, precise, and detail-oriented and yet is also social and sympathetic toward other people. The owner had already been in business for 12 years before launching this division. And he had two partners on the operations side. I realize this guy knew the importance of hiring someone unlike himself to run operations. He is like me: an idea person, a people person, a salesperson. I ask her if she'd be willing to screen applicants for the position she recommends I create—a director of operations to oversee telemarketing, computer support, clerical support, customer service, and bookkeeping. When I walk Chris out of the office she reminds me that the tree in our reception area needs to have the leaves dusted.

May 27: I call Sara K., the board member who is a quality-assurance manager for an international manufacturer. I tell her about Chris H. and this discovery I have made. That I have never hired a manager who is my alter ego—a detail person. She laughs.

She says there is a personality type among operations people. This is nothing scientific, just her own observation. She suggests I go out to the parking lot and look at my employees' cars. If the insides are clean, if those employees are always precisely on time, if they live their lives by a stopwatch, then they belong in operations. I hang up. I can't resist and go outside to the parking lot.

My new bookkeeper's car is sitting next to mine. The inside is filthy: old soda cups on the floor, clothes on the backseat. His office and his work look the same, I am forced to admit to myself. I look at my sales manager's car. It is immaculate.

May 29: I am leaving for a 15-day trip to Italy with my husband and six friends. We have been planning this trip for two years. As the months have passed, I have eyed this date on the calendar and wondered if my company would be ready for me to be staying in a villa without a phone in the heart of Tuscany for 15 days. I decide to leave the company in the hands of Diane, my sales manager. Nancy R., our innkeeper from Cape May, called to tell us she sold the inn but cannot come with us—family problems.

Two hours before I leave the office, Chris H. calls and tells me she is interested in the operations position.

In the flight magazine that I read from Pittsburgh to New York City is a quote I rewrite in my journal: "The best executive is the one who has the sense enough to pick good men to do what he wants done and self-restraint enough to keep from meddling with them while they do it." Theodore Roosevelt. It is another reminder that for our company to grow, I must lead, but I also must hire good solid people to run each area of the company. I decide that is one of the mistakes I have made over the years, second-guessing employees, not clearly defining their jobs, and then not getting out of their way. Determined to follow Chris H.'s suggestions to realign DRM's organizational structure, I draft the new organizational chart and operations job description before we land in New York to catch our overseas flight. I also realize that, realistically, until now I could not afford to hire managers—so I hired people to assist me while *I* ran every area of the company.

June 8: While I am here in Italy I complete the operations director's job description. It is the most thought I have given to a position ever. I realize that in my career, I have hired very few management candidates. Mostly, they have been line employees or supervisors. I call the office once, from a hotel pay phone, and it costs 38,000 lire for Diane to tell me everything is fine.

June 11: Over a long, sunny afternoon I sit with Marion Z., one of our travelers, debating the finer points of running a business. He golfs in Bill's league, and this is the first time I've really met him and his wife, Mary Z. His architectural firm is 80 years old; our business is eight. He shares the company with four other principals; I have none. I do not ask him what his company grosses in a year, but I know he has more than 50 employees and occupies a large space in a premier office building downtown. We talk about what it takes for a company to go from $200,000 in sales to $2 million. He argues convincingly that it is the client relationships built over many years that make the difference.

I point out that I have always drawn a strict line between my business and personal life. When I walk into a meeting with a client, I am the first one to bring the agenda to the table. In fact, I pride myself on handpicking the clients I want to work with, looking for those I like and respect, and rejecting all others. Marion disagrees strongly, and so we debate for most of the day. He feels an owner has to like all his customers and treat them well, no matter what. At night I compare our points and wonder how many times my own beliefs get in the way of my company's growth.

June 16: Back in the office today. While in Italy, I got to know Marion Z.'s wife, Mary. I asked her if she would like to be considered by our new operations person as an administrative assistant once that person is hired. She agreed. I know how she keeps her car, because we shared the same car and villa for two weeks. Morale is actually high when I return. Diane has been solving problems and talking to employees, assuring them everything will be fine.

June 25: The day I got back I posted the operations director's position internally. Diane applied. So did Rick M., my board member. I had sent the description to the rest of the board and the consultants. Today, after discussions with Diane and two board members, I sit with Ruth Ann and carefully ask her to go back to work in the production area. She handles this surprisingly well. I feel an urgency to hire an operations director quickly.

June 26: I meet with Mary Jo K., one of my favorite clients. For the first time, I let her dictate when we will talk about the project. We spend 45 minutes talking about vacations, families, and our jobs. I consider it a superhuman effort not to flip open my organizer to our agenda. I had never realized how prone I was to getting to the heart of a meeting, talking about the subject at hand. We conduct business for less than 25 percent of the meeting, and we part. I am uncomfortable, but as with so many things I have been doing this year, I struggle with myself not to slip back into my old habits.

June 29: I interview Chris H. for the operations position. She sets a salary requirement of $60,000; I have a maximum of $35,000 budgeted for the job. She is coming from a multimillion-dollar company. My favorite advice from my marketing consultant, Jan R., rings in my ears: Hire the best person available for the job. And Chris would be perfect. But I just can't justify the expense. I discuss this with Dwight F. and George S. They agree with me. Chris H. and I do agree that she will work for us as a consultant until I can figure out a way to bring her into the company when we can afford her.

June 30: I have asked Dwight F., who has hired dozens of managers in his 40-year career, to come to my office and interview Diane and Rick M. He spends an afternoon, about an hour with each of them. I am not in the room either time. He leaves before we have time to discuss the interviews, so I call him at home. Dwight says that Diane's experience while I was in Italy has her primed. She wants the job badly, knows our current operation well, and could hit the ground running. Though Rick is a good candidate, Dwight feels he would need six months or more to get oriented to the company. Also, Dwight reminds me that coming to a small company after being a senior manager at a major university might be a culture shock for Rick. That is true. If he needs a new chair, he probably calls Purchasing. If he needs computers, he writes them into the next year's budget. I still consider discount mail-order catalogs to be required professional reading.

I know based on the board's previous advice that they will recommend I keep looking. However, my instincts tell me we need someone now. I hire Diane on a three-month probation and agree to suspend the search to give her a chance to prove herself and give her a chance to see if she likes the job. If she doesn't, I agree she can go back to her old sales position. Six months ago I would have selected Diane purely on common sense and gut reaction. I still reach the same conclusion but feel more relaxed about the decision. The written job description is a first, also. The board never specifically asked for it, but I have a growing sense of accountability to them.

July 1: Tonight I bring my paperwork home in a box with two handles. I did not accept my bookkeeper at the end of his probation, and I am now keeping all the books for the company. I also have to prepare a training schedule for Diane and get our bookkeeping back into some order simulating standard accounting practices before handing it over to a new person. The board is a help, yet I still feel I am out there by myself, really. Diane may be the beginning of a new chapter for us—the first time that I get out of the way and really let employees do what they do best. I also feel this growing concern about the vagueness of my dealings with the board. I am not as "in charge and focused" as I would like to believe I am. Where are we headed? I'm determined, once I slide the operations plates over to Diane's sticks, to begin work on that. And maybe, thanks to the board, I'll begin to scrutinize everything more closely than ever before. I am tired.

July 2: Tonight I pull out the business plan I finished last October with Ed B. from SCORE. It is already outdated. I still don't know what I want out of this business. I need to sit quietly and think about it. Since I've been working 60 to 70 hours a week lately, when exactly do I do that? Bill is going away in September for four days. Decide to take four days off at the same time, go up to our cottage at the lake with the dogs, and write a new business plan.

July 6: Take Sarah K. to lunch. She announced at our April board meeting that she is leaving Pittsburgh and her job as a quality control manager. This is the last time we will see each other. I ask her what she thinks of our company and the board experience. I still hold my breath after those kinds of questions.

She is straightforward. I need to be more clear about what I want from the board. She is right. I haven't really thought through how to best use their talents. And because some of them have never sat on a board before, they wait for me to lead, to tell them what it is I need from them. Then, when they do give suggestions, they expect me to drop what I am doing and act immediately. Adding the board to my life is on the verge of being overwhelming.

July 8: Have lunch with Cathy R., CEO of a manufacturing company that was on the *Inc.* 500 last year. I've been polling people who have advisory boards to see how open they are with them. "I tell them everything," Cathy says. "Why should I hold back? I want them to know everything so they can help me."

I am uncomfortable with that still. After keeping everything to myself for eight years, after never telling anyone the full scope of my deepest fears—not even my husband knows about all the nights I lie in bed chewing on a problem—this idea of verbalizing everything is new and difficult, though I can't put my finger on why.

July 10: Ilana D. from PowerLink calls in response to my memo (did a six-month evaluation of my relationship with the board for my own review and sent a copy to her). We talk on the phone for almost 45 minutes. Why did I need to be told what kinds of questions to ask the board? she asks. Isn't that obvious?

I remind her that the reason I asked for a board in the first place is that I felt I needed help to get "unstuck."

I tell her I am still reluctant to present full financial statements at the board meeting. She is amazed. She insists that financials is the only scorecard that makes sense. That my primary focus and the board's should be how to maximize profitability with the financial statement as the tool to determine that. I counter that my goal is to get help in planning a well-run company in terms of marketing, operations, and management. And that *I* will worry about profitability. She insists I am missing the whole point and that therein may be the key to my problem of being stuck. "If you are not looking at how to maximize profitability, you'd better have a damn good other reason," she says.

I think about the call all afternoon. I respect her opinion and realize what I have been doing up to now has not been good enough. I am willing to shift my focus at least for the remainder of the year. I call her back. Will she agree to be the substitute board member in place of Sarah K.? Ilana agrees. She also recommends I add Larry R., her boss at the accounting firm where they work, to the board. I agree.

July 15: Mary Z.'s first day as Diane's assistant. I think they are going to get along well. Mary will also help keep me in the finance area.

August 10: Business has been building steadily. We have rehired all the people laid off in April. Also set up a more careful analysis of DRM's performance and job profitability. And devised a weird mathematical formula that has been evening out our cash needs. Payroll for two weeks must be at no more than 100 percent of one week's billings or we will be in trouble a few weeks down the road.

Diane N. is becoming more comfortable in her new job as operations manager. She gives me a list of 50 goals she'd like to achieve by year-end. We agree not to initiate a formal marketing program until her three-month trial period as operations manager is over and until her department is ready to handle it.

I sent a meeting agenda and packet of information to each board member (and to my accountant, attorney, banker, financial consultant, insurance agent, and marketing consultant). My accountant calls me today. Will I need financials for the September board meeting? He has never asked me that before. I guess the board makes him feel accountable, too. I accept.

August 24: Mike P. calls. Says his telemarketing friend has a contract that may require our services. It is teleselling, he says happily. That's the idea he suggested at the very first board meeting, in February—selling products directly over the phone. I call. The proposal will exceed $80,000. We'll know in October.

August 25: Lunch with Dwight F. He has referred a substantial amount of business to me over the years. He says I don't need to be so worried about the health of the company. Even after looking behind the curtain, he says he knows I am a good businessperson and that I am responsible to my clients and creative in my work, and he has no doubts that I will meet any objective I set for myself.

I can't tell him how much I appreciate his words. I rarely get that kind of unadulterated praise from an insider. It feels wonderful. I vow to keep his advice and counsel near me for my next depth-of-despair day.

September 1: Third board meeting. Only two board members attend. The rest cancel at the last minute. I am used to this. My regular contacts with the board between meetings are so valuable that I do not begrudge the ones who cancel. I will have my own board next year, though, selected by me. And will pay a small stipend, $50 or $75 per meeting attended.

We go ahead with the meeting anyway because I have a problem I want help with. A woman—Molly P.—has approached me about taking our languishing direct mail operation and building it into a much more profitable division over the next five years, for a piece of the action. She feels she can do $200,000 in the first year and $100,000 more a year for each of the next four years. Am I interested? I ask her to put it in writing for the board meeting.

The two board members think her proposal is thin and that we have not hammered out enough financial details to initiate anything serious.

I am surprised. I like her offer and like her. They arm me with a list of 20 questions to review before I make my final decision. The most important is the one that keeps resurfacing: What is your vision for this company? What do you really want to do?

I admit to them that when I wrote my business plan last fall, I had decided that telemarketing had less competition and better profit margins, and that I enjoyed selling it more. Then, Ilana says, that should give you your answer. Don't do it. Mike P., having been through a rough experience himself, cautions against taking on a partner without getting to know her better. (He suggests knowing a potential partner for at least 10 years.) I don't have 10 years, but I agree to put Molly off for two weeks and to draft a new business plan and a new agreement.

The final board agenda item arrives. We review the financials, and I wait for comments. I get surprisingly few. It is not the reaction I expect.

Hired a new computer person, John, to replace the one we had used for the last year who went back to teaching. He could only give us 10 hours per week, and we needed someone full time in this area. John answered a newspaper ad. He's very quiet, but he came prepared for the interview. He asked the right questions and showed me how to set up the job, without being aggressive about it. He starts immediately.

September 4: We will have our best quarter in the history of the company.

September 8: I leave for the lake, determined to finish my list of personal business goals while Bill is golfing in Myrtle Beach.

September 9: I sit with pen and journal, working on the goals, and then start a list. I tear it up and start over. The goals keep sounding like a business plan for the bank or my staff or the board. Hard to write goals for myself. In some ways I feel the business is bigger than I am. Suppose I decide that my real goal is to live at the lake on Bill's income and read all the Great Books? Suppose I decide that I want to become a rock star? Who cares? I have employees

---

LESSONS LEARNED

#40: Assembling an Interested Board

I've been asked repeatedly by business owners how I found and used my board of directors. It took me almost two years to learn how to best use my board. Looking back, I believe board attendance was poor in the early stages because I was not clear about my objective for it. What advice did I really want? Assembling interested people was the easy part. The idea of helping a growing, interested owner was an easy sell. Now I tell owners (1) know what you want help with and then (2) shut up and listen.

---

who count on me for their livelihood. I have clients who rely on us. I come in every day, work hard until the day is over, and start again the next day.

September 10: I put my personal business goals aside. So that the time here is not a total waste, I write a statement of philosophy about the company. It is the first time I have put a lot of these ideas into words. At least I feel I have accomplished something. I also rewrite the agreement with Molly P. We will do a 12-month trial to see how it works out. If we are both happy, we will spin off the division and she will have to buy in.

September 22: I review minutes from the last board meeting. There are two main things I need to do. First, Mike P. insisted I need to get our accounting computerized and offered to find a local consultant to help us.

Second, the minutes state that "Mike and Ilana were concerned about whether expanding the existing direct mail service fits into DRM's vision for the future." (My new business plan is only halfway done. I've found it easier to write at our cottage by the lake, so I've moved a computer up there. I will take a stab at finishing it the last weekend in September.) But here's the catch: Molly P. has already started with us, on September 17. I know that sounds like the preboard Anita, charging ahead, not doing the necessary planning. Yet I feel much more comfortable with the compromise.

September 23: Sent George G. my diary entries to date. He said he got them but was leaving for Europe and would call me when he got back.

September 25: When I get to the office, there's a phone message on my desk. George called on Saturday. He read the diary on the plane and said to keep writing—he likes it. The magazine will publish excerpts sometime next year. I'm thrilled.

Mike P. has invited me to attend a meeting of company CEOs who meet monthly at one of the most exclusive clubs in the city.

When I walk into the room, I see Barb M., the cofounder of PowerLink and the friend who recommended I apply for the board. She is there as a guest. We sit together and introduce ourselves to the mostly male crowd. Mike also attends. The meeting is a presentation by four authors of business publications. The author getting the most questions is Robert Kelley, who wrote *The Power of Followership.* He asks how many people in the room consider themselves good followers. I am surprised that most of the people raise their hands.

As I sit looking around the table at these men, I wonder how many of them have built their companies by having all the answers. Or how many have let other people come up with ideas that they have listened to with great interest and enthusiasm and then followed. How hard is it, really, to let go of your own company? I order Kelley's book.

September 27: Weekend at the cottage is over. I cannot seem to flesh out a personal vision that satisfies me. I decide to freshen up our mission statement, distribute it to the staff, and get back to work—which is what I seem to do best.

September 29: Meet with Diane M. and Mary Z. It is all I can do to keep my mouth shut and listen. These two women have worked so hard for the company and their employees all week, and they are bringing me up-to-date on their progress. Am I letting them run the company and keeping out of their way? It is very, very hard. I find myself scheduling time outside the office lately. It is easier not to make decisions if I am not forced to confront them. I go on sales calls and take work home to my home office. I read over the reports and think of ways to ask questions without second-guessing decisions.

October 19: I meet with Mike P.'s friend who asked us for the tele-marketing quote. We did not get the job. Our price was competitive and our references were excellent, but his client had gone directly to a vendor without his knowledge.

Over lunch he tells me how he grew his business. (It has become a standard question I ask anyone who owns a business.) It is a fascinating story about a great success and a few setbacks. I do not know him well enough to ask him if he ever sat down and wrote out his personal business goals.

October 22: We are expanding the telemarketing department, and I offer to clean out the area it will move into. In jeans and a sweater, I sit on the floor, sifting through boxes of files taken out of the old sales office. This is where nine salespeople have come and gone over the last eight years.

It's a little like looking at the history of the company com-pressed into "general correspondence." Letters to companies no longer in our market, proposals long forgotten because they were filed by someone who is no longer here. I wonder how a huge com-pany prevents this from happening. Who sits on the floor weeding out sales proposal files at Westinghouse or Apple? Who makes sure all those prospective customers are treated well, not lost in the shuffle during employee turnover?

October 26: Business is going well. Yet my workload seems to be more and more overwhelming. I bring all my paperwork home tonight in a big box. We have more employees than ever, I feel I am delegating more than ever before, and yet I have never felt busier. Can't figure it out.

October 29: In the last week I have received inquiries for our busi-ness-to-business telemarketing that put my lack of long-term objectives to the test. If 50 percent of the inquiries from this month alone turn into jobs, we could expand from 25 employees to 50 employees by the end of the year.

Today I meet with James S., one of three partners in a 12-year-old computer supply company that is grossing more than $1 million per month. He is reviewing our computer needs because we may have to buy more equipment. Yet I cannot tell him how many computers we may eventually need, because I have not decided how fast I want us to grow or where we want to be in three years.

I share my problem with him. He admits that planning for growth sounds good but is not always so easy. Even at a company the size of his, he and his partners work on it constantly. [Note: My board has helped me to open up and share insights as never before. I see that the companies doing $5 million, $10 million, $20 million look and act like mine. The owners are not geniuses or unique by some entrepreneurial definition that could not apply to me. They admit that grave mistakes mark their histories. But they also share great ideas.]

In James's case, he and his cofounders began working in partnership with one of the largest computer manufacturers in the world six months after they formed the company. They have been asking for help from that manufacturer—also a client of ours—and getting it for 12 years.

November 10: Lunch with my banker, Jim S. He is the one who championed my line of credit and equipment loan last fall. He calls me periodically to see "if the patient is healthy." Mostly I tell him about proposals we are working on and new contracts. We are meeting our loan payments easily these days. That feels very good to me. Jim does not mention it. He suggested we hire business students from the University of Pittsburgh to help us with daytime projects. We did that before and found a great employee. I thank him for the idea. (We are in the sixth month of a major newspaper strike, so it is not easy to find people to keep up with our growth. Our turnover rate is less than 25 percent, excellent for telemarketing. Hiring full-time people and paying benefits seem to be paying off.)

I tell Jim we may want to extend our line of credit next spring, based on increased receivables—but that I'd like to see if we can meet payroll without it. The idea of borrowing money still goes against the grain with me. I still don't know how to do a cash flow analysis.

November 13: Mary Z. buys pizza, and I buy champagne. Everyone wears jeans. Lunch is in the conference room, and we stop work at one o'clock to celebrate the past month. Bills are all paid, receivables are at their highest point in the year, and we have two new contracts that could mean more than $250,000 of work next year if the initial tests go well. Molly P. has brought in three small contacts from existing clients for direct mail and has more than $250,000 in pending proposals.

It is time to pat each other on the back. I do not do this enough—let people know how much they are appreciated. We all go home early. I still take work to do over the weekend, but willingly. These are the times when I cannot stop smiling. I feel so lucky to own my own business.

November 15: Finish Joline Godfrey's book, *Our Wildest Dreams.* She touched on a subject that has been disturbing me ever since I started working with the board. I keep wanting to talk about running a good company, and they keep talking about money. I keep talking about empowering employees, and they keep talking about profits. It is a little as if they are speaking Italian and I know only a few words and have to use hand signals. Joline's research among other women in business tells me I am not alone. That is a comfort.

November 17: Mike P. has invited me to my second CEO Club meeting at the D—— Club. The guest speaker talks about negotiating skills. I am sitting next to Cathy R., the *Inc.* 500 business owner I had lunch with this summer. She joined the CEO Club last year and urges me to join. The dues are $1,700, and I have to think about it. I have new chairs, desks, and phones on order. I want to computerize my accounting, which may take up to $2,000 in consulting expenses.

The four negotiating styles the speaker talks about are familiar to me. I wonder if men negotiate differently with women than they do with other men, but in this room of mostly gray suits, I do not bring it up.

One of the business owners asks me to sit at his table for lunch. He may need our services and wants to talk further. Perhaps I can squeeze the $1,700 out of the bank before year-end after all.

November 19: Receive a note of apology from Steve M. He had been immersed in a tough work schedule but wanted to get caught up on the board. We agreed to meet this morning at his office. In reviewing the past four months, I find myself telling him about the lack of focus I have been accused of by the board. It is something I have been wrestling with on paper. If nothing else, I have come to one conclusion in my personal business plan.

To me, the most important thing is to create a growth company that is exhilarating to work for. Growth means I can afford to pay employees better, I can be more generous with benefits, I can provide a career track. I feel that if I can recruit great employees and keep them, we can do absolutely anything! I feel we have that kind of culture now. And I am furiously working on my goal of getting the turnover below 10 percent. (I have continually seen the effects of turnover: systems abandoned when an employee leaves, clients having to be reintroduced, projects having to be relearned, mistakes repeated by a new person.)

Steve listens. I can see he finds this interesting and he agrees with me on one major point—the board doesn't need to be told the entire rationale for my wanting to grow. All they need to know about and help with is the growth itself. I can do the rest within the company.

November 28: It is two days after Thanksgiving, and Bill and I are visiting my family in Philadelphia. Of the four kids, three of us now own our own businesses. We've never really talked about why that happened, but we often use the time together to compare notes. Tonight my brother Ed and I went to visit a family friend, Tom S., who started his consulting firm a year after I founded Direct Response Marketing.

Tom's progress interests me, but I do not want to pry. So instead I find myself talking about my own company. We sit talking far into the night about how hard it can be to make decisions about so many things when you are alone. Tom and Ed ask me about the board. It is still difficult for me to explain this arrangement. No, I don't do everything they tell me. Actually, if I were keeping score (which I'm not), I would say I have followed their advice less than half the time. But what I have overcome is the urge to keep absolutely everything to myself. I no longer consider it a sign of weakness to ask for help.

December 15: At three o'clock today the heart of our computer network goes down. The technician I hired full-time only three months ago, John D., tells me he has called in our equipment supplier but that it doesn't look good.

December 16: I find out that the hard drive on our file server is defective and that we don't have adequate backup to replace the data. Our part-time technician was assigned to do backup the previous four weekends, I am told, but never got around to it. Another Wal-Mart moment, one of those times when I feel for a split second like walking out the door and applying for a cashier's job.

We are sitting in the conference room, the full-time tech, John D.; our operations director, Diane N., and her assistant, Mary Z.; our computer supplier, Bill G.; and me.

As I have felt many times in the past, I hold all the cards. There is no question about who is running the meeting or who will pay the bills when it is all over. If I appear furious or distraught, no one will be able to think clearly.

"So what are our options?" I ask. Bill says there is a company in California that can probably retrieve 99 percent of the data. The hard drive is under warranty and can be replaced. He apologizes for not reminding us to do backups daily after receiving a memo I had sent him a month before on that very subject. John apologizes for not taking the backup more seriously. He knew it had not been done the previous weekend and had just been too busy to do anything about it. Diane and Mary are quiet. They know that they too are responsible.

I realize that no matter how many tasks I delegate, the most important ones have to be clearly tagged by me with fluorescent markers—THIS IS IMPORTANT! Backups? Well, I just didn't say it loud enough.

December 28: We spend all day downtown at a training facility. It is the Monday after Christmas, and I close the office and let voice mail handle the calls while the entire staff meets with me to set our goals for next year.

By the end of the day we have more than 25 sheets of flip-chart paper taped to the walls and filled with ideas. We narrow those down to 70 ideas, and each person takes two goals to work on. It takes a lot of effort for me not to jump in and volunteer to do half the goals, but I decide not to take any myself. Instead, I write down major issues that seem to crop up that will go on my list. Employees want to see regular client-feedback sessions that can be monitored by them; they want more employee recognition; they want more of our policies in writing; they want notice of job openings before we go outside the company; they want to see us send

---

LESSONS LEARNED

#41: The Cost of Bad Decisions

That computer "lesson" cost $4,100 in cash that we didn't have and almost three weeks of down time. Six months later, Michael P. heard about the incident and told me to check to see if it was covered by our business insurance policy. It was. We retrieved everything over our $500 deductible. But the loss of billable time was really irreplaceable. We now do computer backups using an automatic system.

---

out a newsletter that they help with. They have definite and good ideas about how to market the company.

I feel so proud to be a part of this. It doesn't feel like just me alone anymore.

January 5: Tonight is my last meeting with the PowerLink board. Eight people squeeze around the conference table in the room we used to use for meetings. (Last week we installed six more workstations in that room. We also officially rented space across the hall. By the end of February we will be able to handle 84,000 calls a week from our offices. Last January we were at 25,000 a week.)

I finally feel comfortable with these people. I have spent hours and hours in phone calls, meetings, lunches, and more meetings with each of them. We sit tonight with the financials. Our preliminary numbers show that we will hit $484,046 in sales for the year. Up from $367,422 two years ago. Although we have grown by 32 percent, we have not hit my goal of $750,000 yet; but I am not disappointed. We spent the year doing important work—improving operations, training new management, and establishing procedures and quality controls.

Most of the meeting is devoted to marketing. I want to reach a million in sales by year-end. What do I need to do to get there?

We end up talking mostly about the very topic that started the year—focus. I watch eight heads nod. Going from $500,000 to $1 million is a no-brainer, according to Mike P. and Steve M. "Just keep working with the customers you have now and find similar companies in similar markets."

"Did you do a market analysis yet?" Larry R. asks. I'm not sure what that is. "You write down how much business you expect to get from each customer for the year, which determines your budget. Then analyze the source markets and look for like business in those markets." It sounds simple, but I have never done it. Steve offers to help me construct one.

Again, I realize that getting where we are has not taken marketing brilliance on my part. We are in a needed industry. We do our work well. People find us. But that does not make for a great marketing strategy.

For us to keep moving forward, I will have to revive what I did to get from zero sales to the first $100,000: Pick the companies I want to work with and go after them. The sheer determination you get when there are no customers and you are creating something from nothing never really goes away, I guess. We are back to sheer determination, but with more zeros on the end.

The last board member leaves at close to 9 P.M., and I return to my office. I am kind of jarred by their comments, as usual. I listed eight ideas to hit the million-dollar mark, eight different services we could offer in addition to what we already do. They nixed almost all of them. Most of the board members work for major companies, and they look at my tiny firm and wonder why I need help with this issue of growth.

For a moment I see these last eight years and nine months very clearly: I love variety; I love challenge; I am good at executing ideas. So there I am with a bunch of sticks and some saucers ten years ago. I toss a saucer up in the air, catch it on the end of a stick, and start rotating. It is tricky at first, but I catch on. Sometimes it slips and I catch it. Sometimes I drop the saucer and it breaks. Doggedly, perhaps, I keep throwing saucers up there until I have the hang of it. Then I put up a second stick and throw up a . . . dinner plate!

No . . . no . . . no . . . the board is telling me. Not a dinner plate—throw another saucer in the air. In fact, toss up 10 saucers and hire a saucer manager to watch the sticks for you. And find a volume-discount supplier who can sell you more saucers. And set up inventory control of those saucers and get really, really good at spinning hundreds of saucers. *Then you can switch to dinner plates.*

Boring. Too easy. I can feel myself resisting. But slowly and with great effort I am willing to fight this resistance. Someday I want us to have thousands of employees, each part of a team working on telemarketing and direct mail projects for customers all over the world. So for this year, if they think it is that important, I will do what does not come so easily. I will work on saucers.

January 6: I've invited three new people to sit on the board: Burt R., a client and friend, Jim B., a friend who lives near us at the cottage, and Mary Del B., a woman who founded and sold her own employment agency, to replace Sarah K., Ilana D., and Rick M. (Rick got a new job and has less time for us). Mike P., Steve M., and Larry R. have agreed to serve for this coming year. The new board will get a small stipend ($50 per meeting they attend) for the four meetings. This year I want to hit $1 million in sales.

January 8: Darlene and Bill bought a cottage near us at the lake! We are going to see them almost every weekend. Seems so ironic. . . . we have come full circle. Now we really are just friends.

January 11: Went to a spa for the weekend with Barb M., Andrea F., Ilana D., and Sue D. Three of us own businesses. Two plan to someday. We are here to set goals for the year.

Over lunch, I tell Andrea about my experiences with Molly because Andrea is thinking of taking on a partner. Since September, Molly has worked for me as an employee running the direct mail department. She thought she could build it into a multimillion dollar division and asked for some money and a guaranteed salary for 12 months to try it. In a year we would have spun off that division and made her a partner if we like working together.

Unfortunately, in the last five months I've learned that our work styles are completely opposite. When I hear her talk to a client I have cultivated over years and years, I cringe. She dresses like a creative type, I dress very conservatively. She jumps from idea to idea, I like to present an organized strategy. She's not a particularly good salesperson (good at getting proposals, not good at getting signed contracts). As head of the division, that's a major part of her job. I tell Andrea I am glad I decided not to agree to a partnership from the beginning, as she wanted.

January 12: I admit to the group that I want to start a family and that is why I am hoping that Diane and Mary can run all inside operations of the company without my daily involvement. But I see small warning signs. Projects are not going as well as when I was running inside operations, yet I feel if I jump back in, I'll be interrupting their learning process. They'll start to depend on me again.

Andrea says she'll think about what I said about partnerships. This is the second time she is considering a partner, but she is not completely confident about giving up a piece of her business.

January 13: Met with Mary Del B., my newest board member. She founded a multimillion dollar company from scratch and sold it to a hospital a few years ago. Now she works as a vice president at a large corporation. It's hard to find heroes. Women, especially, who have founded companies from scratch. She says she is very, very busy but she will do what she can to attend the meetings.

January 20: Lunch at the D. Club with Steve M. and Larry R. (board). They want to talk about the past year and the coming year. As I wait for them in the lobby, Charlie F., the insurance agent who was one of my first telemarketing clients, walks in, as if right on schedule. We are glad to see each other. "What are you doing now?" he asks. "I own a telemarketing company," I say quickly and tell him where our offices are located. Then his guest greets him and they move down the hall. I turn and find Steve and Larry standing behind me. "That's the first time in a year I've heard you say it like that," Larry says with a smile. "Say what?" I ask. "Say that you own a telemarketing company. For a year you've been unable to describe your business in less than five sentences. This is progress!" I laugh. He is right. Focus, focus, focus. Okay, I'm getting it.

January 26: Went to breakfast meeting of high-tech companies. A venture capitalist was the guest speaker The room is dark as they show case histories of investment and return on screen. They are looking for the next venture. The game again. Another glimpse at this language of business.

January 15: Drove to Cleveland with a colleague to attend a regional meeting of our trade organization. This is one of the few times I

LESSONS LEARNED

#42: The Language of Business

I never took any business classes in college. So when my board started talking to me about basic business principles of profit, growth, sales and marketing, recurring revenue streams, etc., I felt intimidated and uninitiated. Gradually, they kept talking and I started listening. The mystery of their language faded and I began to see clearly what basic elements of business I had been ignoring.

1. *Focus*: I needed to clearly know the business I was in and where my markets were for recurring business. The board always assumed I knew these two things and scolded me when I faltered.

2. *Profit*: I was interested in talking about delivery of service. The board pressed me to pay more attention to the bottom line. As I included profit numbers into my goals, I began to look more closely at pricing, the cost of labor, the cost of benefits, turnover, etc.

3. *Sales and marketing*: The board taught me that it is not enough to be good at going out and selling every day. You have to know the markets you are selling to and have somewhat of a plan of how to penetrate those markets. I finally did sit and write down a plan that I could follow.

4. *Recurring revenue streams*: Probably the most important piece of advice I got was to design new services that businesses could buy over time, not just project by project. We are working on re-tooling almost all our services to follow this model.

have sat with people in the exact same industry. Feels as if I'm at a family reunion. We all talk the same language. I stay long after the meeting is over. I think I finally see what my future can look like. One company is doing $60 million offering identical services. There are much larger companies in the same business. And they are willing to share ideas. I leave wishing I had attended these meetings years ago. The annual meeting is in Dallas in November. I will find the money to go.

LESSONS LEARNED

#43: Trade Associations

Most successful businesses know the business they are in and belong to the trade associations that serve their industry. For eight years I was in so many different businesses, I couldn't afford to belong to all the organizations!

Now I rely heavily on them for networking, advice about computers, consultants, software (this is how we located our current software package), marketing ideas, trends in the industry. It would have also been a good directory of resource people to use when I was starting the business. I think if I had been clear on the business I was in, I would have joined this group in the very beginning at the same time I bought my business cards.

January 16: Meeting with Molly. Sales after five months have not met her original projections. She said it was because she needed clerical support, so I let her hire Kelley R. in December. I haven't even seen a proportionate increase in proposals, let alone actual sales.

I have been here before. My gut told me a few months ago that hiring Molly was a bad idea. But I am finding myself giving her more space, more rope, more time, and new deadlines. I have always found it hard to go against my gut feeling once it sets in. I've also found it hard to do what my gut is telling me to if it involves an employee. We agree on another meeting in 30 days. She says I will see a marked increase in sales in 60 days.

Fortunately, Kelley is a good employee. She could run the direct mail operations if I decide to let Molly go.

February 2: I don't think Andrea is going to enter that partnership agreement.

February 3: Met with Nancy F. She works in human resources for a high-tech company. Over lunch I tell her the problems I've had hiring people, especially salespeople. I've had 9 in eight and a half years. And I want to hire another one. None worked out except

Diane. And she only did it for six months before she applied for the operations director job.

"How big was your net?" Nancy asks. Tiny, I admit. I've hired friends of friends. Friends of employees. Friends. Family. Former clients. Current employees. "Not good policy" Nancy warns. She tells me her rules. Post the job internally (my employees requested that it become policy and we have been doing it). Advertise outside at the same time. Tell internal candidates you must see who is out there, but that they will get first consideration. Sift through lots of resumes, Nancy says.

Look hard. Pay someone to do it if you don't have time.

Time is money. I know it. For now, my time is still free on nights and weekends. But I know she is right. Time to throw out a much bigger net. I post the job internally and advertise in the local paper.

February 9: Second board meeting of the year. First one with new board. This time we skip initial orientation about the company. I have spent hours with each new board member orienting them privately. I use the time to ask their advice about hiring a salesperson. I tell them about my previous bad luck with salespeople. What steps should I use to hire the best salesperson?

They agree with Nancy. Interview lots of people. They agree that some of my compensation plans were inadequate. Straight commission is not good enough. They divide from there. Half feel I should hire an inexperienced person for a lower wage and train him or her. Half feel I should hire a professional and pay $30,000 to $40,000 per year. Michael P. feels I should test first for sales acumen and gives me the name and number of his testing firm.

I don't feel I have any definitive answers. We are in an industry that requires a professional hand. But I don't want someone laden with technique. Our industry has a bad enough reputation without salespeople who act as if they were hungry for a sale. I want someone who knows our industry and believes in it. I feel if they have that, I can train them on the sales process.

I also feel one of my problems with salespeople in the past is that I handed them our service list, price list, and the phone book. I need to give them what we've been giving our clients—telephone-prospected sales leads. We've done this on and off in the past (usually in between salespeople to keep me focused). I could attract a better salesperson if I could tell them they would be getting leads to follow up on.

I write a job description for an inside salesperson. This is a new position. This is the person I will train to generate leads for the outside salesperson I will eventually hire. Before I take any board advice on hiring an outside salesperson, I want to fill this position first. It will be a lower-risk experiment and I can begin to build the sales side of the business while Diane works on operations. I post the job and immediately get four inside applicants. One of our better callers also applies.

February 12: Meeting with Stephanie S. from our self-board group with Barb M. We've gotten to know each other. She owns her own business selling candy and flowers and other gifts to high schools to use for fund-raisers and wants to start selling our services. She is expanded into serving the social service agencies (which is a market we also serve), and wants to start selling our services. She

---

LESSONS LEARNED

#44: Putting Together My Own Board

This was going to be my chance to replace board members who couldn't continue for a second year. My conclusion was that Mike P. offered valuable advice because he had founded his own company from scratch and had built it successfully into a multi-million dollar business. I wanted more people like him on the board. So I added Mary Del B., who founded a temporary employment agency and successfully built it into a multi-million dollar venture. I also added Burt R., the businessman that Darlene brought us as a client, who started a chain of franchise stores, and Jim B., my neighbor at the lake and a savvy operations person. Dwight R. (a client who had turned into a trusted friend and was administrator of a statewide nonprofit), Larry R. (partner in a Big Six accounting firm), and Steve M. (marketing director of a large cultural organization) rounded out my board. I felt that I had experienced people and a few more CEO/founders to share their experiences the way Mike P. had done.

brings up the idea of a partnership arrangement similar to the one I had discussed with Molly.

No, I tell her, I won't do it again now. But I would be happy to pay her a commission if she sells our service to her customers. She agrees and we set up training time.

[Note: Over the years I have gotten used to this. I am approached regularly by people wanting to set up a business venture, a deal, a proposition. But they are designed to fit the other person's agenda. After the situation with Molly that is turning sour as the days go by, I am trying to stick to my own agenda.]

February 20: Filled the inside sales position. Cindy was one of our better callers, been with us since December. I wanted a telemarketer. We did advertise, but no one else came close in background. However the ad wasn't wasted. Diane hired several of the candidates for our operations side.

LESSONS LEARNED

#45: Cracking the Code on Training

I haven't developed anything surefire. But I did get some help from one of my board members, Jim B. He explained that teaching can't be just lecturing. It also must include a measuring instrument so that you can see how much someone has learned. It allows the teacher to evaluate each student in areas of competency. If they are learning business writing, you must assess how well they understand the opening of the letter, proper formatting of a business letter, how to articulate a negative point and a positive point, and how to close the letter. Measuring competency is what has been missing from our training classes for employees.

We are still developing these modules, giving exercises so that employees can measure their own competency in different areas. It is an ongoing process and takes much more time and effort than I ever dreamed. But it has resulted in lower turnover and fewer mistakes and a clearer idea of when an employee deserves a raise.

February 24: Stephanie and Cindy sit in my office while I talk. This is my sales training class. I give them tablets and we all have fresh cups of coffee. I sit back and talk for the next four hours. I talk about our services and how I developed them, about our markets and how they use us to help their businesses. At the end I hand out our price list and we set up the date for the next training. Cindy leaves Steph and me behind to talk.

"What exactly did you call that?" she asks bluntly, which is her style. I laugh. "You don't like my training?" Steph has worked for several large, national companies in sales. She explains to me why I can't teach sales that way. And proceeds to give me insight into how sales training should sound. She said that I am only explaining what to sell. I need to explain how I sell, how I approach different people, what I say initially, what their common questions are, how I recommend programs, how I write proposals, what sample proposals look like, explain how I get someone to move from the proposal stage to the contract stage. I've never had any formal sales training myself, so all I can see is that her ideas will take more of my time to put in writing. But I respect her opinion. She has seen what big companies provide to their people.

I cringe thinking about how I have trained nine salespeople preceding Cindy and Steph. Transferring knowledge. No assumptions. Teach them every single step. What Steph is saying is that I have to take what I know and tear it into bite-sized pieces, writing it down on paper, making copies, and putting it all into a three-ring binder. Steph says she can do it for me, but it will cost over $2,500. I can't afford it.

March 1: I sat with Judy K. She's no longer a caller and has been running our office while also being my assistant. I explain about the sales binders. I am going to do the writing, and she has to help collate and create binders that the salespeople can use. I have been parked by the computer for days dumping everything I know about selling for this company into a computer. So far 50 pages have come out. I used to teach this in one day. I can see this training taking weeks.

March 8: Steph says the sales binder has come a long way, but is far from perfect. It's all bones, no cartilage. It needs connecting pages, explanations which preface forms and samples, sam-

ples of actual proposals, examples. I will fill in the gaps this
weekend.

March 9: Took the car in for service at K-Mart. While they are
working on the car, I am sitting here waiting. It is 8 A.M. and the
place won't open for another hour or so. Yet the whole store is completely lit up, coffee is on in the cafeteria (I got a cup), and they are
in the middle of opening the store. What a process it is! It's clear
that everyone is following an opening process. I am sure there is a
binder like Stephanie's sitting in each department explaining in
bite-sized pieces what has to be done.

A manager walks by me with about 10 people. A regional manager here for a visit? He is walking with them up and down aisles
pointing to signs and explaining how the store should look. Show-
and-tell. A training tool just like what Jim B. would talk about. Do
we do that? Not nearly enough. Perhaps if there is a job for me this
year, it is not operations or sales. It is coach. Walking like that manager, leading employees up and down aisles.

March 10: Met with Diane N. and Mary Z. Told them I can see
something wrong in operations but can't put my finger on it. They
appear tense all the time. So does most of the staff.

I am starting to realize how much training may be necessary
to transfer authority from me to Diane and her operations team. I
tell Diane and Mary I am willing to train from scratch. Let's pre-
tend we just reorganized. Diane says that is not necessary. She will
analyze everything and give me a report. I suspect she does not
understand the real problem. I felt the same tension just before Pat
B. left. Diane may be in over her head. The job is bigger than her
experience. One of my former employees used to say, "First
decide: Do you want to keep them? Then figure out what you have
to do." I definitely want to keep both of them. And I want to help
them.

But Diane and Mary are intent on figuring this out for themselves. In the meantime, my staff is getting restless waiting for
them to learn. Very tempting to step in and make decisions for
them. Will try to hold back.

March 11: Another meeting with Diane and Mary. I will do anything to help you, I tell them. I will review every project, review the

performance of every employee. But they have their own plan. We just have to pay closer attention to everything. And we need more help, Diane says.

I agree to let her promote two callers and let them work five to ten hours per week each as shift supervisors. But it is hard to agree. Between these two employees, Diane and Mary, I am spending four times what I did before when the manager was simply my assistant. They ask for 90 days. They also tell me they want me to reconsider my arrangement with Molly. Her performance and actions are disrupting the office and may be contributing to the tension. This I agree with. I do not want to keep her.

March 12: I meet with Molly and tell her I have to change her direction. I cannot let her continue marketing direct mail services, since low sales indicate that something isn't working. I want her to begin sitting in my sales training classes for our telemarketing division. I also tell her she will be compensated differently at the beginning of April and that Kelley, her assistant, will report to Diane. Molly has been running the direct mail division since September. She agrees quietly and with almost no discussion.

March 17: Kelley's 90-day probationary review. Molly should do it, but with this change I tell Kelley I will be doing it. When we begin, Kelley asks to shut my office door. She then tells me two important things. First, she tells me Molly may be planning to start her own telemarketing company to compete with me. She also makes an important suggestion about operations. If I really want to help the company, I should start sitting in on the weekly operations meetings that Diane now runs [Note: I used to run them until Diane took over the operations job; she said she felt more comfortable if I wasn't there].

March 18: I dismissed Molly. Another detour complete. Back on the main road. As with Fran a few years ago, I didn't offer an explanation and had Judy order new locks. I didn't lose any time off grieving over my stupidity this time. Keep moving.

March 19: I went to my first operations meeting in nine months today. Tried to just listen. Hard. I can see I am making Diane uncomfortable. The rest of the staff, however, is glad to see me. I answer questions, make some suggestions about correcting a problem with a telemarketing project. By the end of the meeting I'm running it. Diane stops talking and looks at me when she is asked a question. But she mostly looks down at her notebook and makes lists. She doesn't make eye contact with me. I realize almost immediately that her lack of knowledge about telemarketing may be affecting her ability to effectively manage my company's operation.

March 29: Traveled to Cleveland to meet with Rob S. who works for one of our national accounts. Rob and I are developing a new product exclusively for his company. This is what I love to do. He is great to work with and good at what he does. We are close to the same age and think alike about marketing. This is what makes owning a company fun. Flat-out creativity and ultimate authority to see through what you have created.

March 31: Our quarterly company meeting. Four times a year we shut down the office and sit in a big circle telling each other about ourselves and our accomplishments. I talk about what we have accomplished and where we are headed. I tell them that if there are questions, there is time for open discussion. No one brings up problems. With 25 people in the room and all the problems we're having in operations, someone would have to be pretty brave. I have to find better ways to learn what is going on.

Removing Molly was good. If anything, I think the staff was upset I had not done it sooner. Everyone assumes I know everything that is going on. Why do they think I keep a crystal ball in my drawer?

End of Year Nine

Years Ten and Eleven: Learning to Grow a Business With a Stronger Foundation

Year Ten

Executive Summary

Type of work:	Telemarketing and direct mail
Number of employees:	35
Business location:	1,500 square feet in converted elementary school
Sources of new business:	Increased phone inquiries from *Inc.* magazine publicity, referrals, repeat business, word of mouth, newsletter, three salespeople
Capital sources:	Growth funded by operating revenue
Average monthly sales:	$60,000
Average sale:	$7,500
Annual revenue:	Approx. $750,000
Greatest challenge of the year:	Having gone against a board recommendation (they said not to hire Molly, that it would take me off course), living with the consequences
Comments:	Molly is gone, and I'm back to concentrating on telemarketing, which is a broad category too if you really scrutinize it. I have to choose those areas of TM where we excel

April 1: DRM's ninth anniversary. When I go into the office I feel all eyes on me. Then I see they have decorated my office with crepe paper and balloons and a huge, white, Happy Anniversary banner

signed by every employee strung behind my desk. The greatest gift: a team of people all moving in the same direction.

April 13: Third board meeting of the year. We review the financials. We have been working with a consultant to get the accounting software running properly. Still have minor glitches. Mary has been doing accounts receivable and payroll since July. She took over payables last month from me. Big relief for me. She is still a little overwhelmed, but she's doing all right. We talk about the publicity pending with the publication of sections of my diaries in *Inc.* magazine. They ask me to keep track of all the sales inquiries and try to not get sidetracked by people who just want to talk.

[Note: this board meeting is being videotaped for a television show for *Inc.* We probably should have scheduled the real meeting for the next night. My attention span is short and I'm uncomfortable.]

April 26: The magazine will be out in a few days. Panic. Why did I decide to be so open about the business? After all these years of being private, I'm telling 700,000 people about my hopes and dreams. I'm going to just stick to business, keep treating every day as if nothing has changed. I wish I could fast-forward to July. Want this all to be over. Had the same feeling right before my wedding.

April 28: One of our clients called. "You are at the airport!" She means my face. The May issue of *Inc.* is out. Diane goes to the newsstand with a pool of money collected by employees and buys all the copies. The phone rings. Another client. Here goes.

April 29: Judy is working part time as the office manager and part time as the receptionist and my assistant. She fields the calls that have been coming in from the story and helps keep me sane.

May 5: I met with Cindy . . . 60 days into her new job. I have a problem. Despite training, the sales manual, and Stephanie's help, I am not happy with her. Why do some people, like Rob and Marie and now Cindy, have a showy temper and others seem to be able to talk about their feelings in normal tones? I cannot tolerate public displays of anger such as Cindy exhibits almost daily. She tells me that she is not the problem—it's operations. She is really talking about Diane running telemarketing, the front office, finance, and the direct mail area. Look closely, she says. You have a problem there. I tell her we will evaluate her performance in another 90 days. Just when we are kicking into gear, I realize I have no backup for Cindy. How many times have I held onto an employee longer than necessary because there was no one to replace her?

Diane's idea to promote Denise and Barb Ma. is a good one. They have a strong handle on client projects—better than Diane, actually. Mary is buried in the finances. We're still having trouble with our Peachtree accounting software, and our Peachtree consultant is taking a leave of absence. Her replacement is not anywhere near as experienced as she is.

May 6: Nancy L., the editor who helped me prepare the diary excerpts for the magazine, invited me to attend the *Inc.* 500 conference. By coincidence it's here in Pittsburgh, at the same time the May issue is hitting the newsstands. There will never be another day like this one. I walk to the registration desk at the hotel and there, on a six-foot-long table stacked three feet deep, are hundreds of copies of this issue with my head on the cover. Amazing and embarrassing. All I did was write a diary.

The weekend is exciting. Being with *Inc.* 500 presidents is like being with heroes—listening to them give testimonials, talk honestly about their successes and problems. No brain surgeons or supermen/women here. Plain folks. Smart, open, relaxed, mostly very willing to share.

I'm a guest, an outsider, a member of the same club, but not in the president's circle. As a member, I'm allowed to ask questions. "Did you plan to be here five years ago?" That's my question; I ask it dozens of times. I'm projecting us five years from today.

"Absolutely not" is the answer. They're mostly people who admit that all they did was work hard with an idea. Do a lot of the right things. But there are no casual members of this president's circle. Everyone has an extra edge . . . a little more ambition, a little more drive, focus, restlessness with today's numbers. Actually, for all these people the *Inc.* 500 is old news. They are working on this year's numbers. Last year was last year.

That I understand. I am no longer the same person that wrote the diary in that magazine. I have moved forward myself.

LESSONS LEARNED

#46: The Affection of Strangers

I was not prepared for the outpouring of affection from *Inc.* magazine readers around the country. Hundreds of people (eventually more than 400) called or wrote to thank me and tell me their stories of frustration and success. One man wrote me a four-page letter outlining all the things I needed to do differently to be successful. Another woman suggested we start a club and call each other as we learn the next step in the game.

My secret fear was that someone would read it and think I wasn't smart enough. I was afraid I had admitted too much, was too honest. That did not happen. There were a few people (less than a handful) who were critical of me. The overwhelming majority admitted that they had made many of the same mistakes. "You are telling my story," I heard over and over.

My only way of giving back all that affection was to return the calls, write some letters, and continue to admit I didn't know everything. If you were one of the *Inc.* readers I spoke with, then I thank you now.

May 9: Peggy G. calls. "Why didn't you tell me? Do you know what I do?" Peggy and her husband own a cottage near ours at the lake. She also works in Pittsburgh and read the article in *Inc.* I laugh: "Okay, so what do you do?" Peggy, it turns out, was a paraprofessional in the small-business division of one the Big Six accounting firms. We set up a meeting with Mary. Peggy has offered to spend a day looking at our books, our internal procedures. Mary is relieved. She has been anxious ever since our Peachtree accounting software consultant went on her leave of absence.

May 15: Jilda A. (a client and friend) throws a "cast party" for our employees, board members, and clients at a local hotel to watch the "*Inc.* Magazine" show. Celebrating with everyone is great. Watching myself on television makes me acutely uncomfortable. As good a production as it is, I am thankful when it is over.

May 30: The month has been a blur. The outpouring of help, attention, and affection from the diary excerpts published in *Inc.* has been incredible. Every day I've talked to people with their own stories to tell, about businesses they have started, lessons they have learned, struggles they have had. I don't even talk about it out loud without getting emotional. I lived my whole life never telling anyone my problems. And then I tell 700,000 *strangers,* as Andrea F. archly points out. More than 200 members of our "club" have called since the May issue was released to wish me well, urge me not to give up.

I try to explain that Part I of the story ended 10 months ago. We are doing much better, thank you!

June 13: Second part of story appears in the June issue of the magazine. No kids yet, but now I know a little of what it must be like to have a second child. Excited, but not quite the same. A little saner. Able to get back to work a little more quickly.

June 15: I feel I have been given a gift. I now know hundreds of other business owners; some are behind me in their growth, some are ahead of me. We can help each other, I am sure of it. How can I repay these people? How can I repay Nancy L. and George G. and Jeff S. (at *Inc.*) for what they've done?

June 16: Fourth board meeting. Not as well prepared because of this craziness from the magazine articles, but told them I had hired Peggy to help us get Peachtree running smoothly. Financials not even ready for this meeting, since Peggy interrupted our routine and is in the middle of doing a complete audit of our books. She says it's the only way to make sure the numbers are right. I can see that a few board members are impatient that we are still talking about problems with accounting. "Just make it a priority and get it done," Michael says. He is right of course. "Be patient," I ask. "I will mail you the financials."

June 24: Lunch with Marilyn V., a business owner who has received a PowerLink board. The article has had an amazing effect on other business owners. It's like truth serum. I can't get them to stop talking! She doesn't like her board. Can't figure out what to do with them.

I understand now what George G. (editor in chief of *Inc.*) means when he talks about the *Inc.* 500 CEOs and presidents of the fast-track companies in his magazine. Once you have gotten to a level of success, everything you have struggled to learn suddenly seems to fit into place and you can't remember what the daily struggle looked like anymore. You can't remember the point of catharsis, when everything comes into focus. So you assume it just worked out that way and you go on. He tried to explain to me why he does so few stories about companies in the middle of their rise to success. While they are in the middle of it, they don't know where they are. Once they hit the plateau, the doors seem to close behind them and they can't remember details as clearly. They can't go back and be dumb again.

Here I sit with Marilyn, struggling to remember how I felt about my board only 18 months ago, and I can barely remember those same vague feelings of dissatisfaction. It's like putting on an old pair of glasses. I ask her as gently as possible if she is clear where she is going. She admits that she's thinking of taking her company in a new direction or possibly running for political office.

I remember it now. Juggling plates, cups, saucers, and serving spoons all at once. Not accountable to anyone. Not having to be consistent because you are too small for it to matter. You believe your employees and clients will follow you anywhere. I try to explain that if she wants to grow, she may have to pour all her energy into one business, then be consistent, disciplined . . . ask the board how to help grow that one division.

She doesn't want to hear this. In fact, she feels more sure than ever she will run for political office.

July 1: Bill and I are taking two weeks' vacation, mostly at the cottage. We go to Jan R.'s wedding in Pittsburgh (she has moved to New Jersey, so our coaching sessions have turned into friendly phone chats; she's no longer in business). Then we head for the lake.

July 9: Have crewed the boat before, and Bill has always been skipper. Now we are at the lake and he is teaching me how to sail. This is the first time I have taken the helm alone. I am petrified. But I've been watching the wind for a year. We sail for almost six hours. By the end of the day, I'm still clumsy but no longer scared. If something happens and I have to skipper, maneuver back to shore, I can do it. Can the distance between not knowing and knowing be this short?

July 12: Diane calls. (She would never do this unless it was something she couldn't handle alone. In my memory, I actually can't remember her telling me she encountered any problem she couldn't handle.) Problem with Cindy. Temper, plus serious errors in judgment with clients. I listen to her description of the incident and then ask to talk to Cindy. Cindy is brief and says she doesn't want to get into it. This is the part I hate. They are both responsible adults. But something is not clear. What did I forget to explain?

July 14: I drive to the office in the middle of this vacation to meet with Diane and Cindy and decide to put Cindy back in operations. She does not want to go back and resigns. Well, at least the office will be quiet. But the tension in the office has not gone away. In fact, while I've been gone it has increased. Something else is wrong. I drive back to the lake with much trepidation and ask Bill if we can go home early.

July 20: I posted Cindy's job again. I have decided that my biggest error was no backup. I decide I'm going to put three people in inside sales. I advertise the job outside. This time we get one great

---

LESSONS LEARNED

#47: When an Employee Won't Admit Not Knowing

Of all human traits, this is one I cannot figure out how to respond to. Diane was just one of several employees who could not and would not admit that they didn't understand something. I used to think it was me. Was I creating an atmosphere that was not open and safe? Did they think I would criticize them if they admitted defeat?

What I finally learned is that confident people admit they don't understand things and people who lack that confidence don't. I wish I could hire only people who freely admit what they don't understand.

candidate and a few possibles. I also recruit Kelley. Ever since Molly left, Kelley has been working on a few special direct mail projects. I don't see her going into telemarketing, and I have effectively eliminated the direct mail division as an area that would be growing. Does she want to apply for an inside sales position? She has lots of sales experience and agrees.

Ever since I got back from vacation, Kelley and Cindy's warnings about operations and Diane's inexpert handling of employees and clients has been ringing in my ears. Twice I've caught Diane crying in her office, yet she won't tell me what is wrong no matter how much I beg. I think she wants so badly to do a good job for me, but to do a good job would require admitting that she needs more help understanding telemarketing theory, and that she needs more effective supervisory skills. (The employees work for her, but her lack of understanding of their jobs appears to be causing them to lose respect for her.)

July 22: Call from a new potential client. I agree to meet with him right away because he's in a hurry to set up a telemarketing program. Dean H. turns about to be only in his late twenties, but one of the sharper marketing people I've met in the city. We agree on a project and a start date in two weeks. Dean says he likes it that we are so responsive. I don't tell him anything, but I don't know any other way to be; are my salespeople this fast? Judy tells me they are not. How do I pass along my unexplainable sense of urgency about everything? Not sure.

July 30: A unique meeting with the president and founder of a major U.S. company. A young woman, Jill A., read the article in *Inc.* and sent me a letter telling me that the secret to growing my company was a strong telemarketing department doing lead generation for our sales force. That's what her company does. I call. She was a telemarketer or inside salesperson for her company and is now in outside sales. Would I like to come up to Rochester and see her operation?

Today was the meeting. The founder and president of the company, Tom G., has also agreed to meet with me. Another club member, president's circle.

Jill sits patiently while Tom and I interrogate each other. Actually, I am more like the young pup and he is the older, wiser dog. I cannot stop taking notes. Tom tells me the whole history of his company. He feels one of the keys to growing into a $190 million publicly traded company was when he united a dozen or so local franchises into a cohesive national organization with sales offices across the country.

At the end of the meeting I tell him about the tension in our office. I feel I must have done an inadequate job of training, and now there are problems. Diane is not really open to more training. "Do you want to keep her?" Tom asks. Absolutely. "Then what else can she do?" She used to work in sales, I explain. Perhaps as long as I am going to hire three inside salespeople, I should also move Diane back into outside sales. Replace myself completely in sales. "Just do something," Tom says, "or your company will suffer. And do it quickly." I weigh this all the way back to Pittsburgh.

I feel I can solve the tension in operations. I have to move Diane out of there.

August 1: The minute I walk into the office today, John (our full-time computer person) asks to see me. He is leaving. Got the job he applied for almost a year before he started working for us (we're his first employer). More money. Closer to what he wants in a job. We talk for a long time. I explain that we're entering the busiest period in the history of the company. By the end of the month, I will be free to work with him more closely in operations. There are going to be some changes.

He is a man of his word. "I already accepted the job. I wish you had told me all this a week ago." We agree that he will continue for us two nights a week indefinitely. He's been a wonderful employee; it will be hard on the staff. Our first fallout from the morale problem we have in operations.

August 5: I hire Laura B. from the outside candidates, move Kelley into sales from operations, hire Phil B. from the calling staff. We will start training in two weeks. It's not fast enough; never is. The sales training schedule is now much longer. It's only worth reviewing if there are more than one or two people.

All three of these people will be in inside sales, prospecting for business and helping me on existing accounts. It's not like the outside sales job, where the only person ever doing it well was me.

LESSONS LEARNED

#48: Morale Problems and How to Spot Them

Someone once asked me how I could have spotted the operations problems if Kelley and Cindy hadn't warned me. The fact was, my employees looked unhappy. They stopped talking when I entered the room. They called in sick. And finally, John quit. Happy employees smile, they give you good ideas, they can't stop talking about their projects. It wasn't so hard, really.

I have also ignored those signs in the past and suffered because I let people be unhappy. I was always sorry later. Just deal with it. I'm still working on this one.

In larger companies, I guess you would have to just walk around a lot to see if you notice unhappiness.

Tom G. in Rochester told me he still has breakfast with line employees on a regular basis to stay in touch with what's going on.

And I was always looking for someone to perform it exactly as I did. . . . As a result, I was never satisfied. How can an owner replace herself, exactly? Its unrealistic to think I ever could.

August 15: To replace John D., our computer person, we are doing what Nancy F., my friend in human resources, recommended, since it worked so well in hiring Laura. This time I ask John to write the job description and post the job on the bulletin board immediately. I also put a classified in the Sunday paper. That generates more than 60 phone calls.

I talk at length to John about what he feels we need to find in a replacement for him. He also agrees to help interview the final candidates. John is going to be difficult to replace. He's one of those rare blends of talent, curiosity, conscientiousness, and a work ethic that comes from solid Hungarian stock.

In the last four months, John left work late every night with a briefcase filled with papers. The next morning he came in early and the work was done. Though he reported to Diane, I hired him thinking he might be the person to run the much larger data center that I envisioned.

When he came to me to say that the government job he'd always wanted had finally come through after two years, I was stunned. I have a policy not to talk people out of job decisions (when I learned the hard way that people who are persuaded to stay end up resenting their decisions in the end), but I broke my rule. I asked him to continue part-time two nights per week. If the cord was still there in a year or two, maybe he could come back in a new position.

Today I interviewed 12 people for the computer job. Tomorrow I have eight more scheduled. Two senior callers, Betsy M. and Joan K., have applied too. They have helped John over the last year and now want his job.

Betsy is the bravest of my employees. When she gets up her nerve, she is the one who tells me what's going on outside my office that I never hear about. Does anyone else go through this? As the owner, I'm outside the information loop. I rely instead on downcast eyes, conversations that stop when I come around corners. I rely on a few people like Betsy who will tell me what is going on if I ask the questions in exactly the right way.

"Why do you always go outside for your experts?" Betsy's question hits me hard. "Don't you realize how much we want to help you? How much we really know?"

In many other cases, she may be right. Even Diane was an outsider. She had never really had extensive telemarketing experience; her background was sales and management. In the case of John, I also went outside.

"Are you prepared to be the last person in the chain?" I ask Betsy and John when I interview them for John's job. "If we get a new system shipped in and it's lying here in boxes, will you be able to put together? If the server goes down and the staff comes running into your office, will you be able to handle it?"

Both Betsy and Joan admit that no, perhaps they are not the best senior person. This time I catch the emphasis. Would they be willing to interview the top three candidates?

I also ask C. W., a neighbor in our building who has gradually become a friend and confidant. Our companies are similar in size and seem to be growing at the same rate. He's a computer consultant and trainer and would be equipped to help me make this decision. As we get bigger, I trust my instincts less and less in hiring. I have made mistakes in the past, and this time I can't afford another. John's job is too important. We have too many projects being managed in his area. We have to make a decision in less than a week.

Betsy and Joan agree that perhaps they're not the right candidates. But I ask both of them to help me. They agree to help interview all 20 candidates. I have decided to only hire someone if both of them agree as well. A single veto, and the candidate will not be accepted.

August 16: Of the 20 applicants, only five seem to fit our needs as far as experience. I ask them back to meet with Mary, Betsy, Joan, C. W., and John. C. W. devises a clever test to let each candidate demonstrate their skills. I only know that one of the questions requires installing a modem. I stay out of the second round of interviews. We do them all in one day. Two candidates will be invited back for a third interview with John and me.

August 20: John's father died yesterday. I meet with the two candidates alone, then talk to C. W. He feels that Greg C. is clearly the best guy for the job. Joan and Betsy agree. Greg and I talk at length. He has worked for a much larger company with much less responsibility and accountability. Is he ready for this? He says he has to think about it and will call me. Can a human hold her breath for 24 hours?

August 21: Greg calls at 10:30 A.M. He knows I'd like him to start today, but would it be okay to start on Monday? He wants to take care of a few things. Relief. I like him. I think he will work well with John. Betsy and Joan both give their thumbs up. He will report to me.

Party at the lake. Diane and her boyfriend, Bob, and Mary and Marion Z. drive up for the day. Haven't talked to Marion Z. in ages. He's considering being on our board next year. Fresh from my trip to Rochester, I ask him what he feels is the key to growth besides building strong client relationships.

He admits that when you have a huge national client, they are going to bring you more business. I can remember a few years ago I thought big companies dealt only with other big companies. But that's not even close to being true. "Anita, you don't need a lot of accounts when each one is bringing in a million dollars apiece," Marion says. I'm getting it. When we first started in business, our average sale was about $350. Today it is $5,000 to $10,000. We need to develop services that generate more revenue per customer. And we need bigger companies as customers.

August 23: Start of sales training. First time using new training binder. Kelley says she wishes she'd had it when she first started with the company. Laura is going to be great too. Phil might not make it. He told me last week he had applied for a job with a huge corporation that could be sending him to Chicago for training. As a freshly minted business school graduate this thought excites him so much, his head spins.

Greg's first day.

August 24: Michael P., my senior board member, called a few weeks ago to ask for this meeting. Mary Del B. comes too. They tell me directly that I have to get the board meetings back on track. What do they want, I ask. Create an agenda and let a couple of people look at it prior to the meeting. Maybe appoint a chairperson of the board to assist with this.

They explain that I am still using the board to discuss issues that are related to daily operations. They want to help with strategic planning. They feel I can handle the daily decisions, such as how to hire a salesperson. They can be looking ahead, helping with the bigger decisions.

Here are two people who do not own stock and get $50 when they show up at a meeting. Yet they have volunteered hours of time and attention to help me as advisory board members. In an unexplainable way, I feel as accountable to them as I do to any one of my employees. More so, I think, because I am not paying them.

Over the last 18 months, I have grown to become much less defensive about criticism from these people. It used to make me angry. Now I still step back a little, but I'm ready. They are right, in a way. Actually their greatest value has been to remind me of the bigger picture. But it has taken me almost a year and half to catch up to them. They outline what the agenda should look like: financials first, then marketing and sales, then operations, and personnel. Then spend the last hour, discussing one major topic. That topic should be reviewed by at least one board member to make sure the topic is phrased in a way that will elicit the most useful discussion.

I also ask them both if they would serve on next year's board. They agree on the condition that I follow these guidelines.

September 1: Meeting with Diane. It is evident at the production meetings that Diane has reached that point I have been in myself: so stuck that you can't be pushed in or out. So I push.

I explain that I'm training the inside salespeople and they will need an outside salesperson to support them. I would like her to return to sales. I'll take over operations. I give her the five-year strategic plan I have been working on. "Look at where we are going, and where you might fit in. There are lots of opportunities. Consider yourself ready to move to the next phase of your career here." No shame in that. For the good of the company, I want her to think about it and let me know tomorrow.

September 2: I have to give Diane credit. She is not a quitter and she's very classy. She agrees to make the switch. We work out new compensation and call a meeting together to explain to the staff what is going on.

After the group meeting, I ask Judy to set up 15-minute meetings with every single employee in the company over the next two days. We are up to 34 now. I want to try to get to the bottom of where the tension is coming from. What do I have to do to fix my company?

After the meetings, my conclusion is, I did exactly the right thing. Mostly what I heard is that Diane didn't seem to understand their jobs and couldn't help with specific suggestions when they had a question. I now see that as her fear of admitting she didn't know how to help them. They saw it as Diane not caring about them. I am running operations, I tell them. I'm paying attention to them again.

September 8: Met with Dean H. again. The telemarketing program was a huge success. He wants to introduce it to the other 120 dealers in his region and wants me to meet his boss, who is in charge of seven other regions like this one. This could be the biggest thing we've ever done; this could be national.

September 9: We go to look at a larger office space. Next year our lease will be up for renewal again. Can't believe six years have passed already. We are looking at a space to accommodate us for the next six years. I have been thinking harder than ever about what we will look like in the next six years. With my strategic plan in hand, it's easier to look at space. It's easier to decide not to buy a building (we can't afford the size of building we will need in five years). It's easier to decide the size we need now; we want at least 20,000 square feet on one floor so that as we grow, we can keep all of our people together.

September 28: Private meeting with Denise and Barb (shift supervisors). One month under their care and my employees are smiling and projects have been restored to their previous performance levels. I have employees coming in to ask me if I saw their numbers from the day before. I feel as if someone hung a sign on my door saying, "Anita is back and everything is okay again." Without really standing on the floor listening to callers or sitting in accounting posting entries or sitting at the front desk answering phones (all jobs I have held at one time), I am running operations. I finally have managers in place who really do understand their areas.

Denise and Barb are running all the telemarketing projects, and I've given them hiring authority (I still approve all dismissals). Mary Z. is running the financial area now that Denise and Barb are really supervising all the telemarketing work. Judy is running the front office and helps manage all inbound projects. She also is my primary ear to the ground. Kelley can handle all the direct mail work. Greg is running the data center, and his biggest problem seems to be that he can be very gruff with the staff and they are afraid of him. But he is trainable and young. I can work with him.

But all in all, I think I have an operations team here.

In some ways though, I don't feel victorious. I feel we are taking a few steps back to go forward. Diane was put through the ringer for almost a year, and so were many of the employees reporting to her. I have to take over operations again and this time do it right. But I also see the importance of staying in sales and working with large accounts like Dean H.'s company. I think I can see the advantage of staying slightly above the fray to work on large accounts, new markets. But I keep being needed on the front lines.

The sales department is down to three people. Phil took the Chicago job, bought a new suit, a new car, and a new pair of snappy sunglasses. I wish him well. Someday soon we'll have our own employees doing that with us after they are hired. Laura and Kelley are in inside sales, and Diane is in outside sales.

I can see Di keeping her distance from the other employees. She has been burying her nose in her work or is on the phone a lot. I gave her most of the active accounts as her customers, since they had been working with her in operations.

October 1: I once went to see a veteran entrepreneur at his office a few years ago. His employees adored him. His office bristled with the energy of a fast-growing company . . . young, energetic, well-dressed people doing good work. No lingering in the halls, whispering. People smiling, moving briskly down the halls. Phones ringing.

Today, our office feels like that, looks like that. (His furniture was newer.)

I can't exactly put my finger on the change. In part, the board had a lot to do with it. I started looking at everything through their eyes. I started appreciating all the hard work of my staff. I started realizing what I had created. I wanted to own that company again. I feel a little like Dorothy in *The Wizard of Oz*: I had the power to go to Kansas anytime I wanted. I just had to be ready. I've been on a trip, and I just came home.

Met with Mary Z. Her job as assistant operations director has completely changed now that Diane is in sales. She admits that since I have her doing all of accounts receivable, payable, and payroll, and working with Peggy G. back in May, she hasn't really been helping Diane. In fact, she admits, she used to help soothe angry employees a lot more and run pass interference for Diane until she started handling our entire finance area.

I guess that explains why this summer has been so tense. Mary admits that she covered for Diane because she didn't know what else to do. Mary's background is really electronic bookkeeping. We agree that she will run the finance area and that she should stay out of telemarketing. I'm going to let my most experienced callers run that part of operations for a change.

October 2: My own favorite expressions drift back to me through my staff now. "Don't bring me problems; bring me a problem and two solutions." "Is anyone dying of a terminal illness here?" (courtesy of Bill) "What's Plan C if this doesn't work?" Ways to think about problems. Tools to use without me being around. Independence.

October 9: Spoke in St. Louis at a national sales meeting of Dean H.'s company. I was there at his personal invitation. This may be the recurring revenue client that Michael P. was talking about. They need our kinds of services on an ongoing basis. I also got to meet with two other vendors who work with this same company. Both men have built companies with this group of dealers as their primary source of business. They have relied on word of mouth and networking and national endorsements from the company headquarters to build their consulting firms. I think we could do the same thing with our telemarketing service.

Dean H. sat down with me over the summer and explained how his company was structured. He said he would help me to become better known any way he could. I can see that our program has made his region look very effective and noticed by his peers. He feels he is repaying me a favor. We could generate $4 million per year from this account. It will take a few years to develop. But I feel that this is the kind of program the board really has been whispering in my ear about since the start.

The program is desperately needed by this market. The program is renewable annually, and there are 5,000 dealers across the country who can buy this program. The company's national marketing office will not officially endorse the program (they told me I was still too small). But they would pay for me to print my marketing materials and would give me good references if any dealers inquired. They said they'd see how we did for the next few years.

October 12: DRM quarterly meeting. Denise was voted Employee of the Quarter by her peers and the employees who have either been working for her over the summer or since Diane moved back into sales in September.

Have hired 10 more people. Sales department seems to have kicked into gear quickly. We are in the stage of growth where figuring out where you are today is a waste of time—the numbers are changing too fast. Mostly the business is coming from accounts I worked on this spring and summer while Diane and Mary were running operations. The three salespeople are exceeding quotas by

LESSONS LEARNED

#49: Where Our Sales Were Really Coming From

There is no question that my decision to focus on a single group of services (in our case, telemarketing) was instrumental in helping us grow. I chose it because I found customers interested in talking about it (more than any of our other services) and I enjoyed talking about it. And as we gained more and more experience and got results for our customers, we started getting repeat orders.

I had to reprint all of our brochures and eliminate mention of all our other services.

I still bump into people who I haven't seen in years and I have to tell them what we are doing now. I wonder to this day where we would have been if I had focused on a single service when I started in business.

But the other reality is that my sales still came from my personal networking and handling of phone inquiries generated from the Yellow Pages, our directory listings, and other advertising. We also started getting more inquiries as a direct result of the *Inc.* articles. My salespeople, though better trained than any other group of people I had ever hired in sales, were still far behind me in sales skill. But with a backlog of work from my previous efforts, I did nothing to improve the situation except to let the new salespeople enjoy their commissions.

I should have done something about it then, but I didn't.

managing my accounts and learning to sell and bring in accounts on their own. In this area, they are still not working fast enough for my tastes. I am thinking we may add two more people by the end of the year.

October 13: Board meeting goes well. Financials are on time and correct. I wrote the agenda the way Michael and Mary Del B. recommended, and I talked to Michael about the main topic: We are working with two national companies and I want to outline the opportunities and weaknesses with each client and see which company they feel I should plow my resources and time into to support and grow. They agree that the one company is experiencing financial difficulty and is on their fourth phase of downsizing. Stick with the other, stable, growing company.

Tonight we spent most of the time talking about next year. It is not December. January is a full two months away. But for the first time, I feel slightly above the fray. We are planning. I have agreed to submit two things prior to the December meeting: (1) a budget of income and expenses for next year, and (2) a list of expenses I think we will incur when we move our offices next year, if everything goes according to schedule.

Again, Michael argues strenuously that we still need to develop programs that provide us with recurring income. That we should stop celebrating our sales, because we are still selling our work one project at a time. It's time to be negotiating long-term contracts. Recurring contracts.

Mary Del says she feels it is the best meeting of the year. Everyone agrees.

October 14: Michael P. calls to repeat what he said at the meeting and clarify. He wants me to understand the value of selling something that continues to sell itself, something that is written into a contract as such. For a long time I thought we had to fashion our service to fit that mold. Now I'm beginning to understand that what he really means is find a market that needs our service so badly that they are willing to pay for it on a recurring basis. I have one client that may fit the bill, one of our national ones. I tell him I'm writing a program and want him to look at it. He's a good man.

October 14: Went to hear Barb M. accept the Athena Award for being an outstanding woman in business in Pittsburgh. She deserves it. Because of her idea, I got my board of directors, which changed the direction of our company. There were 1,200 women in the room. It felt good to celebrate with her.

October 20: Lunch with Doug H. He was the client who challenged my ideas about business and told me that maintaining the status quo wasn't good enough. The company he worked for went out of business, but we remained friends. Like a touchstone, talking to him reminded me of what we were doing three years ago. Was I really that naïve?

Now he's thinking of starting a business of his own. It reminded me of that day in July when I had lunch with Tom G. in Rochester. This is what he must have felt like. Doug's questions were the questions of a novice. "How much would it cost to get a company started like this?" Beginner questions. That day with Tom, I was asking questions (as the owner of a company doing less than $1 million) of a man who was CEO of a company that he founded and eventually took through an IPO [initial public stock offering].

October 24: I talked to an insurance agent today about buying disability insurance to pay the company's overhead if anything happens to me, and to pay me a salary. She projects the premium over 20 years. Oh, I won't need it that long, I tell her. Just for five years.

"What happens then?" she asks. By then the company won't depend on me to open the doors. That's my vision. I won't be in operations. I won't be in sales. I will run the company, slowly stepping back a few steps at a time, setting the pace, the plan, but not really running the day-to-day. The bills will get paid even if I'm only in the office two days a week.

October 25: A woman in our women's networking meeting talked about making a profit with the same contempt I used to show. If there are no other stockholders, what difference does it make? Making money is not bad, I tell her today. In fact, ignoring that number on the income statement is a mistake I made for too long. I don't want you to starve! I am being overdramatic, I know. But she sounds so much the way I used to sound two years ago. I don't want her to make the same mistake. I can tell my advice is not really wanted. I step away.

I guess running a business is no different from running your personal life. When you truly, finally want advice, you will ask for it.

October 28: I rewrite a proposal. I used to write *Proposal by Anita F. Brattina, Direct Response Marketing, Inc.* Now I write, *Proposal by Direct Response Marketing, Inc. Contact: Anita F. Brattina.* I feel as if the company is a separate entity, bigger than any one person, including me. It is an idea managed by hardworking people pitching together. It's not me anymore.

Read a great book called *The Entrepreneurial Myth*, by Michael Gerber. It was recommended to me at our national client's sales meeting in St. Louis. Ron S. says that this book helps you to understand how to grow a business. He says that for a company to grow we have to design an extraordinary service using ordinary people—not brain surgeons—not people so unique they are difficult to replace.

This book intrigues me. I am the difficult-to-replace person at the company. How do I take what I do and strip it down, break it up into manageable tasks that my employees can handle without feeling intimidated? I feel I'm doing that by hiring other salespeople. I put other people in operations. But I still hold everything together. Still not sure how to let go.

Later: I think we got it. I feel like Professor Higgins dancing around Liza Doolittle. Today our operations meeting and sales meeting rolled into each other seamlessly. Everyone was prepared. Reports were accurate and prepared in advance. No excuses at this meeting. Every current project is exceeding goal, and we are above goal in pending proposals. Greg, the new data center manager, was on top of all projects and asked the right questions. I didn't have to cajole, berate, or plead. I feel like dancing.

October 29: Mary is mad because one of the employees messed up a client report that Mary sends with her invoice. "Why can't he be more thorough?" It is a major service and takes Mary hours to correct the problem. We meet. The employee apologizes. He will try not to do it again. Mary tells me that she knows if she did it herself, it would be done right. Probably. Mary is naturally conscientious and thorough. The systems she has created are almost perfect. But instead of agreeing with Mary this time, I think about Michael Gerber's book on the "E" Myth.

I also know that this employee has worked for us a long time and cares as deeply for this company as I do. But he is not, by nature, as organized as Mary. "Did you ever write a checklist of exactly what has to be done?" I ask Mary. She is this employee's supervisor. No. "It's not that hard," Mary rationalizes. "I just expect them to use their common sense."

I hear that a lot from the managers. From Diane. I've said it myself. But maybe that isn't going to work anymore. Maybe we have to do the same thing with operations procedures as we did with the sales training manuals. The operations tasks are deceptively simple, like tying shoes. Hard. Easy. I ask if between Mary and her staff they can write down the steps exactly, in order. I volunteer to write the first document. They can add the refinements. I know they can do it, but they are juggling more than I am now. For the first time in years, I have time.

What else have we been doing that isn't written down? I'm on a hunt to find out.

October 30: C. W., our neighbor in the office building, came over to show me a card his employees gave him. We are both straining to hit the million-dollar mark. As a result, we have been spending hours in each other's offices sharing ideas and comparing notes about employee problems. "Congratulations," the card says, "on hitting your first million." It was signed by all his employees. He wanted to show someone who would understand, and he came to find me.

I was thrilled for him. To have your employees understand and thank you for letting them come along for the ride. To win. To be part of a success. It's what we are in the middle of too.

We will have contracts representing a million dollars, but I don't think we are going to bill more than $700,000 by the end of the year. It's okay. We are on our way. I will miss C. W. We are both moving out of the building next year to larger quarters.

We are members of the same club. You can only get in if you have founded a company from scratch and built it into something you are proud of. The only initiation is the hell you create for yourself. And only you know when you have finally been accepted.

October 31: Dallas. Here for the National Telemarketing Association Conference. Been doing so much traveling lately: Rochester, St. Louis, Philadelphia. Driving into the city from the airport, I pass what seems like thousands of businesses along the way. Who are they? What do they need? How are they growing their businesses? I know we are in midst of pressured economic times, yet I look at these businesses and think about opportunities. Maybe they need us.

I can no longer go back to thinking about doing business within a few square miles of the office. Doesn't seem realistic. Helping clients regardless of the miles. That's how we have to think.

When I was little I used to lie in the backyard and look at the sky and keep turning my head back and forth, up and down, to try to see as much sky as possible at one time. The feeling of bigness would stay with me for days. I couldn't pass a window or go outside without seeing the size of the sky. That is how the business seems now. So much opportunity. So much sky!

The businesspeople I meet do not expect us to be down the street or across the town. They just want to see my face or the faces of one of my salespeople. Then they want immaculate execution. They do not care if they have to fly to us to train our employees or set up the project. For them, flying from Chicago to Pittsburgh is like driving across town. No problem. Fax it, send it via modem, leave the numbers on voice mail, overnight the disk.

Another barrier gone?

November 1: Saw Jim R. at the meeting in Dallas. He's the guy whose operations manager, Chris H., came to our office last summer and drew me an organization chart of how our company should be set up. I modeled my company after his.

I had actually taught Jim how telemarketing worked through a consulting contract almost 10 years ago. Proof again that simply having an idea is not the key to success. It's all in the execution. Jim turned an idea into a telemarketing company with 1,200 employees around the United States. In that exact same period of time we had grown to 40 people. We hadn't really talked in about three years.

He was at our national industry conference to speak and to accept an award, and we had time to sit down and talk. He admits that two years ago he felt he was at a plateau. He felt frustrated. Not passionate about what he was doing. Not focused. I was shocked. Two years ago I was feeling exactly the same way. Only I was doing $250,000 and he was probably doing about $15 million. Can our own inertia and impatience be the same rock that we push off of to move to the next level? As I sat listening to him, I felt comforted. The gap between us seemed very small.

I feel as if I have been on a journey and come back to the starting point, completely changed. I can't go back to who I was. I see the business differently, and I am different in it. More confident. Clearer about where I'm headed. I can see the sky and the ground at my feet at the same time. I am not journeying alone. I am surrounded by people who want to help me get there.

LESSONS LEARNED

#50: Hitting $15 Million

Jim R. figured out from his business experience that a narrow service to a narrow market is the fastest way to grow a company. While I was floundering around locally and regionally offering 57 varieties of marketing services, Jim offered one, learned how to do it well, found other people to help him build it, and eventually was operating in more than 20 states with employees all over the country and selling to national clients who probably were worth $500,000 to $5 million each in annual contracts.

November 2: Marian R. (one of the women who called me after the articles were published in *Inc.* magazine) approached me about working for us. Says she doesn't want to work for her boss anymore. Feels her work isn't appreciated. I imagine what I would say if I were her boss. Did you talk to him about this, I ask? She says the problem is not just him; it's that no one else in the company respects telemarketing and that's her job. I feel I would be stealing her and wouldn't want the same thing to happen to me. I tell her I will think about it.

November 4: I keep pulling back, redefining my role in the company. Lately, I've been concentrating only on the largest accounts and designing new ways to deliver our services. I go to professional meetings and hand out my cards. I get invited to give speeches. I've noticed that our customers seem more understanding that an account manager in our sales department will handle their routine questions.

November 8: Went to Cleveland to meet with one of our two national clients. Diane went in a second car. Good thing because I broke down on the highway. I waited for a tow truck for two and a half hours and missed the meeting. Very embarrassing. But Diane was there with Bill R., our client with this account from the Pittsburgh office. I knew my company was well represented; time for a new car to represent us. For the first time since I started the business, I think we can afford for me to buy a new one.

November 9: Marian calls again. We've talked twice more in the last week. I know our sales force is still not as experienced as I'd like it to be. Did I decide? she asks. Yes, I tell her. I would like to consider hiring her. She will end up making a little less than she is making now, but she will make commissions. She agrees. I tell her to talk to her boss openly about this.

November 10: I've never been here before. I have less to do, but I am as driven as ever. When I look at our major accounts, I see that I am still the one responsible for generating the first contact through referrals, word of mouth. I develop the projects to a certain point and then one of the inside salespeople takes over. Their job is to keep the client happy and turn the work into more business. I can see that Kelley, Laura, and Diane are still not able to juggle as many tasks as me. And none of them is capable of bringing in a large account purely on her own. I still feel that no one in the company is as driven as me. That is hard to watch.

What I really need to do is stop nitpicking. I need to let my staff (who are really very competent) do their thing and spend my time developing more accounts.

November 12: I tell everyone that Marian will be joining us as our fourth salesperson. I'm still looking for one more.

November 13: Marian calls me. Her boss doesn't want her to leave. He counters with a $10,000 raise. I don't even consider countering his offer. First, he clearly needs her. Second, I would not hire her as an equal to the other three salespeople and pay her more money. It wouldn't be fair. I wish her good luck. Marian thinks we could still work together as their vendor. I call her boss. He says he was angry with me. By the time we are done talking, he is okay. Actually, he'd make a great board member someday.

November 29: Bill took me to see a beautiful house for sale. We aren't looking for a house, but this one is great and mortgage rates are low right now. Proof that sales can have nothing to do with logic. We fall in love and rationalize our purchase later. We are going to make an offer.

December 6: Ginny C., friend and former client, has joined us, doing administrative work part-time and in the evenings while she looks for a job. She lost her job in July and has been looking for work ever since. She had a bad experience and feels burned out. Not the first time I've done this. I feel lucky that I'm in a position to offer. Plus, she has wonderful public relations and fund-raising skills. I don't think we can afford her full-time. But she had a bad experience and she just needs to coast for a while. She's reporting to Greg and doing some overflow computer work to help him out.

December 19: A week before Christmas. Our house offer was accepted. We will close next month. The bank is processing the mortgage in record time. They said it was easy since our business and personal records are up-to-date. I credit Jim S., my banker. He always reminded me of what was important to keep in the files. Plus, Jim is on our board, so he also receives quarterly financial statements. I gave out raises to all the key managers and myself. The salespeople are making good money since I've been giving them all my accounts. My income has also increased to $1,000 per week and I may raise it again after the first of the year. I finally feel that the business can compensate me, but it has taken almost 10 years.

December 21: DRM Christmas party. Judy's idea was to have it at the town community center. Judy, Bill, and I went early to decorate. Everyone else went home to change, dress up, bring their favorite dish. The center had a huge stone fireplace, and Bill kept the fire roaring all evening. Through the bank of windows along one side of the room we could see the 50 candles we had lit and set outside on the deck. It was magical.

December 22: Year-end meeting to review the books with accountant John S., Peggy G., and Mary. Peg has a hard time with Mary's "controller" skills. She has 30 years of accounting experience, and Mary only has five. She keeps expecting Mary to understand everything she says. Mary is demoralized from the daily pressure by Peggy. I agree at the meeting to let Mary hire an assistant. Mary says that will help smooth out her area and make it less stressful. I agree. Besides, Peggy told us that after the first of the year she is going from part-time to full-time in her day job and can only work with Mary on evenings and weekends.

Peggy will help with the interviews. We took Michael P.'s advice and bought the small accounting software program he uses. Peggy installed the program he uses in less than three weeks. It is running smoothly. Mary will run an ad this Sunday.

December 23: Called Tom G. (the CEO from Rochester who met with me last summer) to say hello and ask him a question I've been struggling with. I still feel tense and overworked. Why is that? He says that I'm probably doing someone else's job or I'm supervising too many people. I'm only supervising eight people, so I must be doing someone else's job.

I'm still in sales (I still bring in the majority of the accounts, but the salespeople handle them and get the clients to continue doing projects). I'm still in operations (I still solve problems). But I'm not sure what move to make next.

December 24: Christmas Eve with Bill and his family. Then we drive over to Mary (S.) and Gary's for dinner. Lots to be thankful for.

December 27: Our annual company meeting. This year Joan K. is in charge of planning it. We always divide the staff into four groups (customer service, employee satisfaction, operations, and sales and marketing). Then everyone meets once before the annual meeting in their teams to review the goals we generated at last year's annual meeting. What did we accomplish? What do we want to accomplish in the coming year? Each team makes a presentation at the annual meeting. Then we spend the rest of the day putting ideas on pieces of paper taped to the walls. We end up with over 150 ideas and then narrow them down to 50 goals. It will be our working list for the rest of the year. The biggest problem seems still to be the hand-off of projects from sales to operations and the need for more training.

December 30: Still working on an accurate list of our moving costs. With this move, I want to give each caller even more space, acoustic silencers around them to give them more quiet to make calls, more comfortable chairs, better-quality headsets, and a phone system that can accommodate the growth. I think we could do $3 million to $5 million in the new space. The cost to move could exceed $100,000. Oh my goodness.

January 6: This year I also resolve to travel lighter. I'm carrying a small pocket calendar like Mike P.'s. No more thick organizer that I carry around like armor.

January 10: Mary's assistant started today. Mary Ann G. will work 20 hours per week and help Mary with coding all bills and entering them into accounts payable. She will also help with producing the financial reports. But I know Mary's intent is to teach her how to do everything. And that isn't a bad idea. Mary and her husband, Marion Z., Bill and I, and four other friends are going to Italy again in June for two weeks. Total backup in finance will protect us. And now that Peggy is working full-time at her other job, her consulting job with us is really done. We will really need Mary Ann.

January 20: We are definitely moving this year. The office is so crowded, we have to tape a piece of bright yellow paper on the wall in the telemarketing office when the bathroom is occupied. Otherwise, people would be popping up every five minutes to check the bathroom door, which is two offices down the hall. I asked Stan F. if I could rent more space on another floor, since our floor is loaded to capacity. Between my neighbor, C. W., and us, we've gone from employing 20 people six years ago to employing more than 75 people. We can't even stock enough paper towels in the bathroom to last the entire day.

January 30: Stan is reluctantly letting me rent 400 square feet smack in the middle of his offices on the third floor so that three more employees can occupy my old office on the first floor. There is no place in his office for me to sit after his employees leave because they want to lock up their area and turn on the third-floor alarm system. They can't do it until I leave. Since I'm used to working until at least 6:30 P.M. at work, this is tough for me.

But I'm the only one who can move without disrupting company operations. The rest of the company is on the first floor. We

---

LESSONS LEARNED

#51: Financial Help

It was only after working with Mary Ann G., Mary Z., Peggy, John S., our accountant, and Mike P. for a few years that I began to understand Mike P.'s recommendation: We need someone really sharp in finance. That investment can help protect me.

Mike feels we will eventually need someone full-time who is like a controller, reviewing financial reports, able to make recommendations and notice trends, spot errors in pricing or double billing issues, etc., and who can produce new financial reports and recommend new ways of looking at our finances. Mary is the first to admit she is not of that caliber. Mary Ann has the skills, but not the experience. Also she only wants to work part-time. Peggy has the right background and experience, but we can't afford her.

Recently I met a woman who ran and built a business for a man who owned an automotive aftermarket company. She's a bookkeeper, like Peggy, with an incredible amount of business savvy, street smarts, and common sense. She gave me examples of how she tightened her boss's operations and created systems for analyzing the important numbers. That's the kind of person we will need. Mary has the bookkeeping skill, but she can be soft and let people get away with exceeding 30 days before paying us, giving out discounts too easily, letting the salespeople talk her out of making a collections call to one of their clients. Mary and I have talked about this many times, and she knows that eventually we will bring in someone over her in that department.

Mary Ann is much tougher, more objective, but she works part-time. We are going to need a really tough, objective, experienced finance person as we grow. It will be the best way for me to protect what I've built.

---

picked up two national accounts last year, and one local client is giving us more work. We are billing $25,000 per week.

February 5: Goal-setting retreat at a nearby resort for my business networking group. There are 22 women business owners here, and I can see the pain and struggle some of the people are going

---

LESSONS LEARNED

#52: Going National

It was because of all the business owners who called me after the *Inc.* magazine article was published that I became confident enough to work nationally. I ended up corresponding with more than 400 business owners around the country who had no problems considering doing business with me. It opened my eyes to the possibility of working nationally.

But the way we got the national accounts still started locally. It was because I called on the local sales office of these national companies and did successful local projects. Then I started talking to the regional manager, national manager, . . . and so on.

---

through. I remember those struggles so well. I try to explain that some of the struggle isn't necessary, but I feel as if my words were falling on deaf ears. "You don't understand," I can almost hear them say, "You've made it to the other side."

February 9: Even after talking to these women, there is a part of me I don't share with others. There is a part of me that understands and craves a simple life. Live in the cottage, drive a used car. Managing a company, employing other people, taking the ultimate risk, putting our mortgage on the line every day are hard and stressful.

February 11: Talked to Jill A., the young woman who invited me to visit her company in Rochester. She was one of the people who called me after she read the article in *Inc.* She really wants to leave her job and start her own business. She's about the same age I was when I started this business. What advice do I have for her? I end up writing her a long letter and tell her:

1. Starting out with no money is okay. It will make the game very clear from the beginning. You are like a seed growing in a rock garden. You'll have to figure out how

to grow by finding enough water (money), enough light (money), enough soil (money). You will live by your wits.

2. You need to be very clear about what you are selling. That was probably my biggest mistake. Every time you change your mind, you lose some customers and you lose your focus.

3. Stick to very narrow products and very narrow markets. This was another big mistake I made. I thought I could do any kind of marketing and sell it to any kind of business.

4. When you hire people, tell them your goals. They'll help you achieve them.

5. If you change your goals, don't drag everyone around behind you if the first idea is working. Hire new people to work on the second idea. Otherwise your employees will get disoriented.

6. If you are good at sales, hire someone to run the office. If you are good at developing the product, hire someone in sales. But know that if you have to hire a salesperson, unless you are really lucky and hire exactly the right type, you will probably struggle. If you can take the plunge and learn to sell yourself and figure out how to do it, you will always be more successful. Then you'll know operations and sales, and you'll be able to teach replacements for both.

7. Spend ten times more time on training than you think is necessary. No one ever gets it as fast as you did.

8. Plan to grow your company large enough to have an office and place you can lock up and go home. Plan to grow big enough that other people can make up for your weaknesses unless you happen to be one of those rare birds who are very, very organized, a very good salesperson, very good people manager, and someone with boundless energy and highly disciplined. They are rare, and when I meet them they are usually older and have had plenty of time to work on themselves.

9. Don't get too enamored with the idea that if you produce a great product, the world will beat a path to your door. That is true in rare instances, but mostly you also need sales and marketing.

10. Most new businesses underprice themselves. Pay some-
    one to do competitive research for you if you have to.
11. Always look for ways to increase your average sale. The
    larger the account, usually the more profit there is in it.
12. Look for ways to repackage your products to guarantee
    recurring revenue (like selling maintenance agreements
    with hardware). If you analyze most successful compa-
    nies, they either have a few huge accounts keeping them
    going, or they have a recurring stream of revenue based
    on how they bundled the services.
13. Set up a sales system. Salespeople are notoriously unfo-
    cused and disorganized. Give them weekly and monthly
    quotas and make sure they meet them.
14. Take a class in cash flow analysis. Understand how your
    company makes a profit.
15. Talk to people who own successful companies, and ask
    them lots of questions.
16. Read good books to develop yourself.
17. Put together a group of advisors who have some distance
    from the company and who can advise you. Make sure
    one of them is a CEO who founded a company from
    scratch and built it to at least $5 million in sales.
18. Set up formal reports that emphasize the numbers and
    ratios that are the most important to you.
19. Know the important ratios in your business, and watch
    them daily or weekly.
20. Learn to inspect your personality closely. What are your
    private weaknesses? They will become the weaknesses of
    your business.
21. Big companies employ average, everyday people like you
    and me. Make them your clients. They have money and
    are hungry for good services. They go to your church,
    shop where you shop, and stand right next to you to buy
    fertilizer at Hechingers'.
22. Accept the fact that making money is a primary goal. Try
    to understand your personal biases and negative
    thoughts about money and wealth. They will interfere
    with your ability to make money.
23. Use a payroll service. Get a computer, fax machine, 24-
    hour-a-day voice mail, and a cellular phone. Stay in this

century, and use these inexpensive tools to leverage your time and provide faster customer service.

24. Put your company in the Yellow Pages and pay the higher phone rates. It is how some of your biggest accounts will eventually find you.

25. Hold regular meetings with your staff, and remind them of the things that are most important to you. Reward them for work well done.

26. Hire new people on 90 days' probation at a lower salary and no benefits until you find out what they are made of. Then raise their salary and give them benefits. If possible, even start out hiring them part-time to save even more money. It is the only protection against a bad hiring decision.

27. Assume your time is worth $10 per hour in the beginning. Then move it up to $20 per hour, etc. Hire people to do things you are doing at less than $10 per hour. For example, if you are starting out alone and you are doing everything, should you hire a salesperson who could eventually make $40,000 per year ($20 per hour), or should you hire a secretary, receptionist, bookkeeper, or office manager instead and pay them $9 per hour? Always choose the second. It is cheaper. And ideally, hire them to start part-time.

28. If you are barely meeting payroll and you don't have high enough receivables, your pricing is wrong. If you are barely meeting payroll and your receivables are at least three times your payables, you just need a line of credit to borrow money for one or two weeks until the receivables come in. Note: receivables are booked orders already invoiced. It is what you are doing this for.

29. Continue to be a good friend, mother, wife, and daughter outside of work. Own pets, learn to fish or golf. Read. Preserve your other life.

30. Never think you are alone. Figure out what you need and seek help; don't tell everyone your life is great when it isn't. You are surrounded by people who want you to succeed. It is a natural reaction. Take advantage of it instead of hiding from people.

Jill, I tell her at the end of the letter, if I think of anything else, I'll write it down and send it to you.

February 14: I am still a bottleneck at work. Why? I still approve all the bills before they can be paid. I still handle the major accounts (time to assign salespeople to each of them with me). I still get reports from 12 different people and meet with 12 different people regularly. (Can Judy help me put all these reports on a single piece of paper, as I used to have years ago?)

Working on a new bonus program for all callers plus writing an operations manual and starting a team leader college with regular classes during off-peak hours for staff.

February 17: George G. (editor in chief of *Inc.* magazine) says that as people get more successful, they forget what it took to get started. I was talking to our women's business group about how to grow a business. In the room was a woman whose business is only a year old and she is struggling. I talked about narrowing her market. "How do you turn away business?" she asked. I realized that I was telling her to do what I said, not what I did. I hardly ever turned down business and never turned it down in the first five years.

March 12: This has been a difficult winter. We lost lots of billable hours due to six or seven weekday snow storms, and the freeze/thaw has caused the office to flood. Today four of my employees are working with their feet in water for the third time this year. Stan, the landlord, has retired to his condo in Vail and his people in the building couldn't care less about us. My staff is working in damp offices while the landlord's office manager has never even walked downstairs to see the damages. Ever since the floods I've been carrying my tote bag of work downstairs from my third-floor office and worked at an empty desk in the flood area so that I could see what the workmen were doing (or not doing).

We are very close to signing the lease on our new space. Marion Z. (Mary Z.'s husband and now, finally, a board member) has been a big help. He's been talking to the owner of the building on my behalf, since they are business associates. My attorney has the lease, and hopefully we can move by the middle of April.

I've asked Judy's daughter, Michelle, to manage the move. She's home from college for four more months before starting a master's program. We are going to buy all new work desks and dividers, some additional computers, install new computer wiring that is more reliable, and put in a larger phone system. We have quotes from everyone, and it looks like I will need to borrow about $50,000. Then we can pay cash for the other $50,000. I am a little nervous, but not much. We are doing good work, projects keep rolling in. Especially from one of our national accounts.

March 18: Tonight I had dinner with Sue D. (a friend who joined our annual goal-setting retreat last year). She told me about a woman in Pittsburgh who helps Americans locate and adopt orphans from Russia. I'm part Russian and part Armenian. The thought that our children could be somewhat the same nationality makes this decision even easier. Bill has agreed to look into it with me. I can't believe it. I feel this is our answer to starting a family. According to Sue, we could adopt two children before the end of the year!

March 21: Office move delayed until the end of April. House move delayed until the beginning of May. Am I nuts? But good things are happening too. Receivables are higher than they have ever been. Payroll is met easily, and we are paying our bills. We can actually buy some of the things that we've kept in our "to buy when we have extra money" folder.

I am running the company differently. There is something amazing that happens with two experienced people working in each area instead of one. I have two people running telemarketing, three people in sales, two people in finance, two people running the office, two people running data processing. The synergy of two people bouncing ideas off each other, using each other as a sounding board, has taken the heat off me. I can see how we could get to $3 million or $5 million or $10 million in sales: Narrow our product line even more, focus on vertical markets, add more salespeople, keep promoting from within, keep on training people on how to do things well, keep turnover to a minimum.

End of Year Ten

Year Eleven

Executive Summary

Primary services:	Telemarketing, telephone research, telephone fund-raising
Number of employees:	40 plus 20 temporaries
Sources of new business:	Telephone prospecting, direct mail, and direct sales in five selected markets
Capital sources:	Increased line of credit to $100,000, and $53,000 long-term note from bank to partially fund move to new offices. Rest of growth funded through operating capital.
Average monthly sales:	$90,000
Average sale:	$10,000
Business location:	6,500 sq. feet in five-story corporate office building. Our neighbors are regional offices of Fortune 500 companies.
Annual sales:	Approx. $1.1 million
Greatest challenges:	Controlling sales, redefining my goals, and experimenting with letting go

April 3: I will remember last year as the year we finally made some money.

April 5: Walt Disney Studio's president was killed in a helicopter crash. But the industry analysts recommend continuing to buy stock because of Team Disney—a deep bench of solid managers who can absorb and handle the loss, and because the chairman of the corporation knows everything that is going on. The customers and the employees and the stockholders are safe because the company is not one person. The responsibilities are shared. I think we are getting there.

April 19: We get a call: The furniture won't be ready until the end of May. We will have to move over Memorial Day Weekend. I hit the roof and chew out the furniture salesperson. With an order this large, she could have warned us when we placed the order. I have been so careful in the last year to never do anything alone, always include my department heads in meetings and decisions, and wait for their recommendation. When I get the note on my desk I ignore the request by Michelle, my employee in charge of the move, for a meeting and instead call the furniture store and demand an explanation. Judy walks into my office with that look she sometimes gets. Sit down, let's talk. As it turned out, my entire management staff met for hours after the call came in from the furniture store, deciding the best way to respond to the news. They called vendors and the landlord and got commitments from employees to work over the holiday weekend. After 10 minutes of listening to Judy explain what they had done, I was embarrassed. They are better than me in some ways. I am sorry, I say. Thank you.

Letting go feels strange.

May 7: My friend Barb M.'s moving company is helping with both the office and our house moves. This weekend was the house move. There is plenty of space for kids and dogs. With this move, I can't work at McDonald's to support my mortgage. The business is now the center of our lives, and my commitment to it has to be unwavering. I felt, as I walked around this new house, as I did with every office move we've made: a little sick, because I am consciously taking us through a gate. On the other side is more commitment to the business, less opportunity to be flexible, or to back out of the whole deal and live at the cottage for the rest of my life being a hermit. Is it possible to take on all this debt and still have a balanced, serene life? I hope so. That's my goal, anyway.

May 15: Had lunch with Mary Del B. (board member). She asks me about my vision for the company. I tell her I see us as being worldwide one day, but maybe not in my lifetime. I also admit that I'm really not exactly sure where I'm headed now. I'm so thrilled with the idea that we are finally able to pay our bills and have the phone ringing, I don't want to move out of this light. She asks me about my level of ambition and seems disappointed. Then you aren't going to take it to the limit right away? she seems to say. She happens to work for one of the most ambitious CEOs in the region. Am I losing an edge, a drive I used to have?

I decide after rolling the conversation around in my head that every owner has to find the level of commitment and debt and responsibility and control he or she is most comfortable with. For example, right now I still feel I run every aspect of the company. But as my employees get more experienced, as we get bigger and attract more experienced people, I think my confidence in our ability to sustain future growth will change. I will not wonder if we should grow. The business will naturally grow because I will be free to concentrate on fewer areas. I've noticed that we have grown every time I felt confident in letting go of a key area.

LESSONS LEARNED

#53: Knowing What You Want

Every time the landscape changed, I saw the future from a different vantage point. Today, I want a solid company that I can manage, using good staff working from a single location. I think we could grow to 150 or 200 people, with 25 percent of those in administration, and be highly profitable, doing maybe $4–6 million in gross sales and concentrating in certain markets. Now that we are in year eleven, I don't think I want to take the company beyond that level. Our services might alter slightly, our markets may change, but as long as I'm clear on what I want out of it, I think we will be okay.

I also decided that for me, it's okay to change my goals as I go. Because I am changing, experiencing different things. It's a natural part of running a small business. Knowing that I am adopting two children and running the business simultaneously, I have to be careful to stay balanced. The business needs my vigilance, but my family will need me too. I need to create a company that can allow me to do both well. And that means a company I can manage on 40 hours a week, with only a little travel, good, solid managers and salespeople, clearly defined markets, and products that create recurring revenue.

May 25: Lunch with Larry R. (one of the original PowerLink board members). He couldn't make the last board meeting, so we are having lunch at a restaurant in his building. I explain what has happened over the last 18 months—this act of letting go. He is thrilled, and we celebrate. We've come a long way together.

I am at a new level as far as running the company with this board. I want their advice, and yet I find myself needing it less and less. For now, they have helped me wade a wide crossing. They told me I had to sit down and put in writing who we are and who our markets are. I did that, and they were right. It made a difference. They told me I needed a sales force, and I have trained three people on how to bring in new accounts without any involvement from me. They told me I needed to be out of operations, and I have trained that staff to bring in projects and help them through the whole process down to the final billing without me. Work can be contracted, done, closed out, and billed, and I don't even see it except on a report. They keep adding layers and layers of experience and quality to their work. And this experience can't be duplicated through training.

Thanks to the board, we have a great relationship with the bank, and a new accounting system that gives me the reports I need to manage. We will have a new office that can accommodate three times more work.

May 27: Went to my first board meeting for PowerLink (the organization that gave me my first board of directors two years ago). Sue D. is the current president; she called me a month ago and I've agreed to serve as president next year. Barb M., one of my best friends and cofounder of PowerLink, is still on the board. We grant advisory boards to qualified women-owned businesses. The meeting is devoted to reviewing the work being done with three companies that received PowerLink boards in April. A lot of the problems sound so familiar. Mostly the business owners are afraid to talk honestly about their business problems and fears.

May 28: In the 48 hours between Friday and Monday, a life can change irreversibly.

On Friday we closed the doors to the office we've outgrown in the last six years, and on Tuesday (Monday is a holiday) we will open as a new company. We are not the same anymore. There is still a part of me that is petrified. There is no going back. Our lives are hurtling in a new direction. A part of me is greedy for more, and a part of me wants to freeze the picture–just stop and relish what we have.

June 1: New offices. Most everyone comes a half hour early. I swear a few people are wearing new clothes. The sun pours through the bank of windows that I have been dreaming about for six years. Our rent is double what we were paying at the elementary school. But I feel we are starting a new chapter here.

June 5: We are in Castellina in Chianti, Italy. Arrived hot and tired from two days of travel. We have rented the villa until the 18th. When we came here two years ago, I spent an enormous amount of money calling the office only to be told everything was fine. This time I gave Judy our phone number and told her to call if there were any problems. I don't expect a call. Mary Z. is with me, but Mary Ann is covering her department and she's completely up to speed. She knows the manager of the branch we bank with if there are problems. I can't think of a problem that could occur that our staff couldn't handle. I think calling would be an insult.

The reason I was so angry about the delay in our office move was that I was nervous at the prospect of being out of the country after only three days in the new office. But the office staff was preparing for this for months. The move was flawless.

I've changed into fresh clothes and I'm going to join the group for dinner on the back patio. I relax.

June 19: First day back in the office. I spend most of it in meetings, hearing about every decision that was made in my absence. My role, I can see clearly, is to congratulate them on their good decisions (which all of them were). The differences in the company over the last two years (since our first trip to Italy) are incredible. I left with contracts in hand and running smoothly and at least 110 percent of goal. The combined DRM experience of my sales force is eight years. So there isn't a question that would come up that one of them can't handle. Judy can handle any operational issue not directly a telemarketing problem because Denise and Barb can adeptly handle that area. Greg and his assistant, Matt, do a fine job in processing and managing the computer system. Every client has an account manager assigned to them. Pricing is consistent and standardized, so I know that no job will be brought in underpriced. So this is the company we have wrought. My job is to keep looking ahead, hiring good managers, training, networking, and enjoying what I have created.

June 25: We got our final bill for installing the new phone system. I hit the roof! Tom D.'s quote (from the phone equipment installer and service company) in February was for $20,000. That was the number I used when calculating costs and getting the bank loan. His final bill came in at $36,000. It is the third time I have visibly lost my temper in the last five years, and two of those times were over this office move. I called him and asked for a meeting to review the bill. When he came in, he said that the original $20,000 was just an estimate and that it had taken a lot more time. I could barely speak I was so furious. I asked him for a detail of every bill vs. the estimate and who authorized the additional expense. I had Judy call some other dealers in the Yellow Pages. No other authorized dealers for this system in the city. We are over a barrel. He didn't even apologize.

July 3: Tom finally came in with the details on his bill. I reviewed it with everyone involved with the move around the conference table: Judy K., Mary Z., Greg C. Most of the charges were not authorized by anyone. His rationale was that I was impossible to get ahold of, and he didn't perceive Michelle as a decision maker. Then I really lost it. I accused him of taking advantage of me, Michelle, and the company. I agreed to pay for all the equipment, but not the extra labor. He said that he would not service the system until I paid the bill. Standoff.

These are times when I hate being in business. What I really want to do is never do business with him again and tell the next 50 people I meet to stay away. What I know is that I did not get a "not to exceed" contract that we both signed. He has taken advantage of us in an area where it is hard to switch vendors without yanking out the phone system. Now I know he is not to be trusted, and we also found out no one else in the city services this system except him. At least for now.

July 8: At our production meeting I calculated our contracted hours and weighed it against pending proposals likely to convert. We may run out of major projects by the beginning of August. Salespeople have been occupied with managing the large contracts we've had on the floor for the last eight months (and, I think, relaxing a little knowing they had commissions coming in). The board says I should lay off staff. But I think that will send the wrong message. Layoffs have a deeper effect than the savings in payroll. Our receivables-to-payables ratios are still excellent. I'm going to put every nonbillable hour into prospecting for new business for the company. Let our staff help us bring in more contracts. The salespeople are digging in to help too. We will get through this.

The other reality is that our salespeople really have been living off of "house" accounts—the ones that I brought in and nurtured and they have taken over. They haven't really learned aggressive skills in staying on top of proposals and getting contracts renewed quickly and effectively. I still have lots of work and training to do in that area. And maybe it is time to hire a really experienced salesperson who knows how to bring in major accounts and keep them happy. Someone who is management material.

July 9: One of our national clients is about to have another round of layoffs. One of my favorite clients from the company, Bill R., could lose his job (though I doubt it; he is one of their best salespeople). He'll know at the end of the month. In the meantime, I want the sales force to be experienced and trained and have my full confidence in their abilities by the end of the year. That's when I plan to leave for a few months after we adopt the children. I have moved Ginny C. from administrative duties into sales. She joins Diane, Laura, and Kelley and has been concentrating on our nonprofit accounts, which is her speciality.

July 25: Met with the social worker from the adoption agency a second time. She says we can select our children in a few weeks.

July 30: Bill R. didn't lose his job. Another sales group picked him up. It's time to talk to him seriously. Bill has sold products and services of $100,000 and more in a single sale. He's the person I would trust to represent me if the president of a Fortune 500 company called and wanted a presentation. He is one person who would make me nervous if he went to work for a competitor of mine (the best litmus test of whether you should hire someone, I was told once). I know what he is making. If he would agree to higher sales quotas, I think I could afford him.

He feels he could generate $1 million per year in sales for us. But he insists he needs to be assigned very narrow markets and be handed very narrow products to sell to them if he's going to hit the $1 million mark.

August 23: Lunch with Irene S. last week. She has a PowerLink board and a multimillion dollar company that has been struggling lately. I catch myself asking Michael P.-type questions: How did you build the business to this point? Where did you get your leads for new business? Who sells for you now? Where do you want to take the company? Do you see yourself in sales or operations? Who is doing the other? Are they any good? Why did you choose this product? This market?

I could barely answer these questions myself three years ago. And most people who are struggling can't answer these questions confidently and knowledgeably.

August 24: We know who our children will be! A little boy and a little girl. Possibly by the end of the year.

I have to choose the areas of the company where I am really the most important.

August 28: One of our three salespeople, Kelley R., is on probation. She has not met her sales numbers for three months in a row. This is her last month, and then I have to let her go. She refuses to take responsibility for generating new business. She is blaming her lack of sales on the fact that not many phone inquires have been coming in over the last four months. I explain that her job is to prospect and not wait for the phone to ring. It is hard to manage someone who won't take responsibility. It is another quality I have to look for when I am interviewing.

August 29: Here's how I am spending my time now: I do very little writing of proposals (in fact, all of my accounts have been assigned to one of the salespeople, including the national accounts). I read and analyze reports, including our 401(k) contract with the bank and our new employee handbook. I no longer write the paycheck newsletter (Joan K. is the editor, and she does a fine job—better than I could do, actually). I review the new salespeople's proposals and the major proposals. I have been the primary teacher in the training classes we've been holding for employees all summer. When this series of classes is done, I want to start a new series but teach fewer classes. It will be my way of staying connected top-down in the company. I am selling less than I ever have in the past.

August 31: I ask my people "What do you need from me?" Usually they want to just talk, bounce an idea off me, ask me for money to buy something that will help them do their job better, or facilitate a meeting between two departments to help resolve a problem.

The company is small enough that I can walk around and see everyone. (I purposely put my office smack in the middle of the telemarketing area and usually have the door open so I can see what is going on.) I also am in a lot of staff meetings and client meetings, but Judy and I share the calendar so that she can schedule the staff when they want to sit down and talk about something formally. I prefer that over being interrupted several times a day because I spend so much nonmeeting time on the telephone.

The telephone is my lifeline. I keep in touch with 10–15 people a day in addition to my meetings. It is the way I keep throwing out the nets. I like that that is my job. I'm still the person responsible for finding out what customers need, meeting new people, developing new projects. Whether I'm working three days a week or five, I feel that should be my primary role. And Judy K. and Mary Z. keep their ears to the ground and let me know the minute there are any problems or rumblings on the floor.

In our current offices with our current equipment and resources, we could be generating $3 million to $4 million in annual sales. I could manage that similarly to how I'm managing it now, I think. Larger than that, and I will have to find new ways to manage. But I don't know for sure.

September 7: Bill R.'s first day at work as our fifth salesperson. (We moved Ginny from administration into the sales area over the summer.) Since we have worked with him for the last two years as a client, he already knows everyone in the office. In fact, we even bought him a mug with his name on it because he came in so regularly. Now I can't believe it, but he is finally part of the staff. And he already had a list of people he wanted to call on. We meet to discuss objectives and he says he's ready to skip the training and just make presentations. We agree that we will go on a few together, but he already knows the company. In fact, he was instrumental in selling our services within his company for the last two years. In his old job, he was accountable for bringing in $2.5 million in sales each year. He has been assigned three markets on which he will concentrate his energy.

September 15: Kelley gave her notice. She got another job. Thank goodness. She was on probation for low sales and I was going to have to let her go. Her last day will be the end of the month.

September 23: Today, Barb E. gave her notice. She was one of our best callers. But here is the frustrating thing. Marian R., the woman who wanted so badly to work for me last year . . . stole her from us! She met Barb when we did a project for her company in the summer. She called Barb at home and offered her a little more money and a chance to earn larger commissions. I was furious for the third time this year at being taken advantage of. I think what was so difficult about this is that Marian pretended we were good friends and even hired us to do work for her boss. That's how she met Barb. When I found out, I immediately called Marian and asked her if she wanted to explain her actions. She said, "This is business, Anita." I told her that is not how I do business. She reminded me that I was going to take her away from her employer. I reminded her that she approached me about the job; I didn't approach her. When I reminded her of this, she was quiet for a minute and then said, "This is business." I told her I didn't want to do business with her or her company again. And then hung up. I am still fuming. Then I changed our contracts. No one can hire us and take one of our employees for three years after the contract end date without my consent. Thank you, Marian.

September 24: Had lunch with Ron L. from my CEO Club. He founded a huge company that distributes office equipment but only works there two days a week. I wanted to know how he did it and asked if we could have lunch to talk about it. I'm committed to cutting my hours next year to raise these kids without hurting the company. He said that the key is good managers and good reports. After I told him how we were set up, he said it sounded as if we would be just fine. In fact, he sounded as though he could have used some of my reports himself. Anyway, it felt good to compare notes. He also concluded, I think accurately, that my role in the company is really as sales manager. I'm the cheerleader who watches their performance. I go on calls with them. I give them

---

LESSONS LEARNED

#54: The Role of the Owner in a Small Business

Six months after this published section of the diary ends, I experienced major problems in the sales area. We reorganized again and let two people go. One was Diane, who had been with me for almost four years. The core problem was that when I spent less time in sales, it had a ripple effect on the department. The reality was that Kelley's sales were low because I had stopped handing her accounts. The same thing happened to Laura and Diane several months later.

It was thanks to Bill R., our newest and most experienced salesperson, that I realigned sales around Bill and me as the primary outside people. We now use inside sales only for clerical support and fielding very basic questions and smaller accounts (under $5,000 in value).

I have in Bill someone who can handle major account selling, possibly even better than me, which is a breakthrough for the company. For that talent, I have paid more in salary than for any two salespeople combined. But it has been worth it. If I get hit by a truck, the company won't shrivel up and die as it would have with just my old sales force.

The other reality I had to face is that I will always be in sales. And proportionately, the more time I spend with major accounts, the bigger we will be. Because after all these years, I am still the company's best spokesperson.

So I'm committed for the next three years to staying "in the market" where I belong for the good of my customers, my employees, and my family.

leads. I help them close. He's right. That's what I am, and that's what I will continue to be.

Finally, he admits that when he founded the company, he hired a guy who was a fantastic sales manager for another office equipment company. The guy really ran the company as if he owned it. Ron L. just acted as an investor and guide and chairman of the board.

Oh. Hire good people. I get it. But I also think Ron was a little bit lucky. He found a great person on the first draw of the cards.

September 26: The last two months of really slow sales have pointed out that we need a focused marketing plan (not just Anita networking in the business community). Bill R.'s suggestion to focus on select markets needs to be in writing. And we need another sales report. Bill R. calls it a pipeline report. Basically it is a running list of all outstanding proposals with a value attached to each proposal.

When a proposal turns into a contract, it is removed from the pipeline report and must be replaced by new proposals. So they report to me on their percentage of pipeline goal every week. If they need $150,000 in the pipeline and they have $200,000 in the pipeline, then they are at 125 percent of goal, etc. Had we been doing pipeline reports this summer, I would have seen that we had an insufficient supply of proposals likely to convert into sales.

We used to do something like this years ago, but I never asked salespeople to add up their list of proposals and compare it to a monthly quota.

September 30: Today is our open house in the new office. Ginny C. pulled it together, and the employees pitched in and brought desserts. The office looks wonderful, and I have to pinch myself a little. We are in one of the nicest, newest office buildings in the eastern suburbs, we have a great staff, we render wonderfully useful service to our customers. We are large enough that we can afford to take time out of our days to train and encourage our staff. I was hoping we would hit $2 million this year, but our July, August, and September lull is going to prevent that.

I have to say I'm very worried about sales. I still am the primary locator of major new business.

I think Bill is capable of being my superior in sales, but that may take six or eight months. In the meantime, this year we will probably do $1.1 million. We have a business plan that will carry us over the next few years. We have an office and systems that will hold for the next few years.

As people come into the open house, I greet them and watch them exclaim. Some of our guests remember the office when we were in that old hotel with the dirty hallways. Some have only known us since we have been in these pristine offices. In the middle of the open house, I get a phone call from the adoption agency. It looks like everything is a go for us to leave for Russia in two weeks.

Another new chapter is starting.

I heard this at a party. A successful businessman is being interviewed by a reporter. "What is the secret of your success?" the reporter asks.

"Good decisions."

"And how did you learn to make such good decisions?"

"Experience," the man says wisely.

"And how did you get your experience?" the reporter inquires.

"Bad decisions."

End of Year Eleven

Epilogue

We finished the year at $1.125 million, and we brought our daughter, Katerina Michel, back to the United States on December 22. The second adoption, which was to take place in October, never occurred. We got the call a week after the office open house. We are still trying to adopt a little brother for Katie.

The employees presented me with a plaque of congratulations when we hit $1 million at the end of October. The board members pitched in and bought me a beautiful bronze plate celebrating this benchmark. My mind, however, was on a poor fourth quarter and my struggles with how to turn five people of varying sales skills into an effective sales organization. Especially if I intended to work only four days a week and spend more time at home raising children.

I believe very strongly that even if we take a few steps backward, we will still keep growing until we get to the optimum size. I think we are still searching for ways to repackage our services into recurring revenue programs. The staff I have assembled can manage us up to $5 million in sales. I know more clearly what makes a good employee (mostly because I've made so many hiring mistakes). I have a core group of good, solid customers. We do very, very, very good work.

I still don't think I have completely figured out this great game of business, but I haven't met a successful founder who thinks he or she knows it all.

If you own your business or are considering it, I hope you can avoid even one mistake by reading through this diary. I wish you well.

Welcome to the club.

Acknowledgments: Cast of Characters

If I had written a how-to book of business suggestions, perhaps this list would be shorter. But this is my diary. I am hugely aware of how much the business has been affected by the people around me. So I would like to acknowledge these people for their support over the last 11 years. I also wanted to create a reference list of the characters who appear in the diary.

In alphabetical order by first name:

Alexandra Stoddard, for showing me a better way to do it all

Alice Nourie, for her gentle spirit and gifts as a writer

Andrea Fitting, a fellow businesswoman and recipient of a PowerLink board

Aram and Lucy Fayda, for their parental support, love, and guidance

Arlene and Howard Smith, for their great loyalty and toughness as businesspeople

B. J. Leber, one of our first clients for "Welcome to the Neighborhood"

Barb and Albert Mastrogiacoma, for their humor, skills, and dedication

Barb and Carol Ehrenfeld, for working hard and laughing often

Barb Moore, for stepping in at most of the critical junctures and leading me down the right path and for becoming one of my dearest friends

Betsy McDonald, for being a critic when critics got no rewards

Betty Horvatin, who taught me it is better for the economy to pay someone else to do it

Bill Brattina, my incredible husband and companion and advisor in the middle of the night when no one else was listening

231

Bill Curry and John Novasel from Triad Litho, for looking the other way when we took 90 days to pay our bills in the early years

Bill Kernick, a business owner, who kept me plugging when I felt down

Bill Reight, a great client, a better employee, and a patient friend

Bill W., owner of an advertising agency in Cleveland, who gave me some help in my first year in business

Bob and Bean Mientus, for talking about owning a business in college and planting a seed of an idea

Bob DeGusipe and Lee Clair, clients, who gave us our chance to enter the world of networked computers

Brian M., one of the original DRM board members and a CPA

Bud L., DRM telemarketer turned salesperson for about one year

Burt Rice, one of our first clients, a DRM board member, and a friend

C. W. Kreimer, our aggressive, sometimes annoying, but always inspiring office building neighbor

Cally Vennare, a wise friend and client

Carol Miller, the banker who helped with our debt consolidation loan

Carol Moran, our production coordinator, who tried valiantly when I didn't deserve it

Cathryn Connolly, a friend and colleague, who keeps me on point

Cathy R., CEO of an *Inc.* 500 company, who counseled me in year eight

Charlie Ferrara, a client and the person in charge of one of the most successful insurance agencies in our region

Chris H. (fictitious name), operations director of a large telemarketing firm

Cindy G., inside salesperson for DRM in year eight

Colleen and Mike Ruefle, employee (Colleen) and client (Mike) and friends

Darlene (and Bill) Smith, one of my first employees, who believed in me and taught me what is really important in life, and who has turned into one of the best sales and marketing people I know

Dean Howell, for being the initiator of our first national account and for teaching me what a dedicated employee looks like

Dee Dotter, my colleague, who formed the Women's Business Network, which enabled me to finally feel comfortable and supported by other women in business

Denise Morgan, daytime telemarketing manager, hired by Diane
      N. and an incredibly loyal employee
Dennis Unkovic, for good advice!
Diane and Ed Yarosz, for their kindnesses and for teaching me
      there are 50 different ways to measure intelligence
Diane Nystrom, salesperson, operations director, and friend,
      friend, friend
Doug Henneman, operations director of an environmental com-
      pany and, eventually, friend
Dwight (and Ruth) French, board member, client, friend of
      Darlene Smith, and, eventually, dear friend
Dwight Reichard, who taught me enough to give me the confi-
      dence to start this business
Edward Fayda, my brother, my confidant, and a business owner
      in his own right
Edwin Blum, my SCORE counselor, who became a friend long
      after my plan was accepted by the bank
Eileen Fayda, my sister, my best friend, a former employee, and a
      great graphic designer
Elena Fayda, who taught me when I was a little girl to never, ever
      give up
Ellen and Michael Martin, our sailing friends
Ellen Ruddock, for unflagging support
Ellice Jackson, for being the first truly successful saleswoman I
      met on this journey
Fran M. (fictitious name), DRM's first telemarketing manager
George Ator, colleague, for teaching Barb and me how to speak in
      public
George Gendron, for reading his own mail, and for calling first-
      time authors in their offices at 6:30 P.M.
George Steinbrenner, who told me about his business in
      Cleveland when I was getting started and helped me along
      many times after that
Georgia Trusio, for being a great supporter
Geraldine Bown, colleague, who proved that you could own a
      business in the United Kingdom and encounter the same
      challenges
Ginny Caliguiri, a wonderful friend and loyal employee
Greg Churley, a great employee, who taught me that being hard-
      nosed is not always bad

Holley Grant and Bill Bailey, our Nova Scotia friends, for showing us there's more to life than business

Ilana Diamond, colleague and cofounder of PowerLink, the organization that granted me my board of directors after seven years in business

Inc. readers who called, sent cards, notes, letters, and support—a very large thank you!

Irene S., who received a PowerLink advisory board

Jacqueline Flynn, an editor who bravely read the whole story with me

Jan Cook Reicher, client and marketing coach, who proved you can even conquer New York City if you put your mind to it

Jan Grice and Don and Olivia, for being good friends even when I said nothing

Janet Sikorski, our second telemarketing manager

Jay Anweiler, for her unflagging dependability and humor at work

Jeanne McNutt, a dear friend, who helped us bring Katie to the United States

Jeff Seglin, from *Inc.* magazine, who had the original concept for this book and supported me until it happened

Jesus Almendarez, who taught me how to lead gently and with great wisdom and humor

Jilda Apone, a friend in the truest sense and an ardent fan when I seemed to need cheers the most

Jill Arena, the young sales rep who invited me to Rochester to meet her boss after the *Inc.* article was published

Jim and Carol Brown, friends, and a board member (Jim), who made me debate my business ideas out loud so that I finally began to share my ideas without fear of judgment

Jim Gilmore, for his unflagging belief in me

Jim R. (fictitious name), owner of a large telemarketing firm (Chris H. worked for him)

Jim Stager, banker for DRM, who got us our first major loan when the business plan looked better than the business

Joan Kennedy, a DRM employee, who taught me that every adversity offers an equal opportunity for inspiration and success

Joe and Mickey Brattina, Bill's parents and the people who taught me what principles and discipline and integrity really mean

Joe Brattina, Bill's brother, who taught me how to ask, "What did I just learn from this horrible experience?"

Joe Gater, for his steady stream of advice when I first learned to ask for it

John Denes, employee, the first truly reliable computer expert who could explain our system in terms I could understand

John Novotny, one of the first business owners to give me a consulting contract

John Sundin, CPA, for providing stable advice in my worst subject: finance

Judy Koontz, my secretary, my left hand, my sister in spirit, and the greatest helpmate anyone could wish for

Judy Pearlman, for showing me you can be an astute businessperson and a great mother

Kara Anthony, my PowerLink support person, who helped me through the first year of board meetings

Karen Brattina, my niece and friend

Karen Reinhart, mail supervisor and hardworking employee

Katerina Michel Brattina, my long-awaited daughter

Kate McPhee, business owner and friend

Katherine Goth, my grandmother, my mentor, and the first business owner I met in this life

Kathleen Levinson, for her kind support and helping hand in the maze of big-business selling

Katy Shultz, client, great businesswoman, friend

Keen and Karen Almendarez, for friendship and for giving business ownership the humor it demands

Keith Crytzer, a client, who gave us our first lead-generation project for a major U.S. bank

Kelley R., DRM inside salesperson

Ken Judson, for being a great attorney and gamely following me on this journey

Kirk and Laurie Haldeman, for being great clients, a board member (Kirk), and friends

Larry (and Julie) Fayda, my youngest brother and a man who knows exactly what he wants

Larry Lagattuta, sales rep, baker, and man of many talents, who helped me get one of our first large contracts in the history of DRM

Larry Ranallo, one of the first board members and a loyal supporter

Laura Berberich, DRM inside sales rep

Lee Ann Munger, for her thoughtful advice on this manuscript

Len K., one of our DRM salespeople

Linda Dickerson, an amazing colleague and founder of the CEO Club, which allowed me to share ideas within a network of successful male counterparts

Liza B., vendor turned friend, turned DRM salesperson, turned ex-employee

Lyn and Joe Decker, friends and a founding member of our self-board (Lyn)

Lynn and Alan Mandel, for helping a young company in a pinch one Thanksgiving when it mattered

Maggi Mansfeld, one of our first salespeople, who taught me what cold calling really was

Marian R. (fictitious name), who wanted to work for DRM, with unhappy results

Mary Ann G., the able assistant Mary Z. hired to help in her department

Maribeth Coote, a client who believed in us and helped us get our first major fund-raising project

Marie B. (fictitious name), temporary employee and friend of Lyn D.

Marilyn V. (fictitious name), woman who received PowerLink board

Marion Zentarsky, a thoughtful board member and savvy businessman

Mary Culbertson Stark and Gary Stark, dear friends and supporters

Mary Del Brady, DRM board member and dear friend

Mary Glenn, a patient, direct, and kind editor and champion of this project

Mary Jo Killian, one of my favorite clients and a good friend

Mary Zentarsky, bookkeeper and the best vice president a president could have

Matt Doll, an employee who taught us all how to operate our computers through a great sense of humor layered over computer knowledge

Michelle Domeisen, a friend who is one of the sharpest women in business I know

Michelle and Tina Koontz, who helped me with the move (Michelle), for their independent spirits and contributions to our company

Michael Pierce, board member, who played a critical role in mentoring me for the last four years in business and who forced me to stop making excuses and think logically

Mike J. (fictitious name), production manager at DRM in Year Three

Molly P. (fictitious name), direct mail department manager

Nancy Furbee, human resources specialist, who befriended and advised me for a few months

Nancy Lyons, from *Inc.* magazine, who taught me what gentle editing, good pacing, and a clear voice really mean

Nancy Rishforth, for being an innkeeper and a business owner, who shared her frustrations—and for being a friend

Pat Brattina, my sister-in-law, bookkeeper, and office manager, who made sure I made it through the first seven years

Pat Olivo Lang, my first client, who asked me why a person of my background would want another job when I could open up my own business

Patricia DiVecchio, a colleague, who teaches balance in business

Patti J., a DRM salesperson and lover of all wise writing

Peggy Grajcar, accounting specialist and neighbor at the lake, who offered to help us switch from Peachtree to new accounting software

Phil Boxwell., superstar insurance salesperson (worked for Charlie Ferrara)

Rae Gold, for her ability to be an artist and a businesswoman

Rich and Maria Barron, dear friends and supporters, who also referred business to us

Rick M., colleague and board member, who applied for position as operations director at DRM

Rita Petkunas, for showing me what it really means to be a dedicated employee

Rob Hanlon, a patient and wise advisor and attorney

Rob M., DRM employee who ran customer service department

Rob Scanlon, a loyal client and a fellow writer

Rod S., DRM salesperson for a brief time

Ron Linaburg, executive and friend, who helped me look at running a business part-time

Ron Monah, for gentle advice

Ronnie Hughes, for knowing when to swing and when to run

Ron Smith, consultant and colleague, who helped me understand our national account more clearly

Rosemary Launikonis, who is the spirit of entrepreneur and
woman blended together very, very well

Ruth Ann Butler, assistant to Janet S., who ended up running the
department when Janet was on leave

Sandy Brown, a gifted writing teacher and fellow diarist

Sarah Kalil, a wise board member in year eight

Sara Kaiserian, for teaching me when I was a teenager that
women business owners could be tough and elegant at the
same time

Scott Neely, a client from the bank, who helped me get one of our
largest bank projects

Sharon Wilson, for her help as a client and a friend

Shirley Goldstein, who always gives her advice straight from the
shoulder

Stan Friedberg, our second landlord at the converted elementary
school

Stephanie Schrass, who advised us on our sales training binders
and joined our self-board for one year

Steve McCloskey, board member and friend

Sue and Morris Balamut, for being there, by phone, 24 hours a
day

Sue Krzeminski, for being a young college graduate who raised
my hiring standards

Sue DeWalt, a fabulous attorney, a great friend, and the one who
led me to my children

Suzanne Caplan, for her wise guidance as a fellow author

Tom and Shelley Sammartino, business owner (Tom) and longtime friends

Tom D., telephone equipment supplier during our move to new
offices

Tom F., a client, who gave us our first major telemarketing
account and wanted to become a business partner

Tom G., the CEO in Rochester and a patient advisor

Welcome to the Neighborhood, DRM business program in early
years, sent to new residents

Wendy King, for being wise, wonderful, and as close to a mother
as a friend can be

Books Worth Buying

The E-Myth, Michael Gerber (Harper Business 1990)
Getting Organized, Stephanie Winston (Warner 1991)
The Great Game Playbook, Jack Stack (Doubleday 1992)
Growing a Business, Paul Hawken (Fireside 1988)
How to Get Control of Your Time and Your Life, Alan Lakein (NAL-Dutton 1989)
Living a Beautiful Life, Alexandra Stoddard (Random House 1986)
Money Is My Friend, Philip Laut (Vivation 1989)
Our Wildest Dreams, Joline Godfrey (Harper Business 1993)
The Power of Followership, Robert Kelley (Doubleday 1992)
The 7 Habits of Highly Effective People, Stephen R. Covey (Fireside 1990)
Swim With the Sharks Without Being Eaten Alive, Harvey Mackay (Morrow 1988)

Note About PowerLink

For those of you who feel you would like to start your own advisory board, feel free to contact PowerLink, which is still an all-volunteer organization, through my friend:

PowerLink
c/o Barbara Moore
305 Jefferson Drive
Pittsburgh, PA 15228